Fish of
Colorado

FIELD GUIDE

T0126167

by Dan Johnson

Adventure Publications
Cambridge, Minnesota

DEDICATION

To my children, Jacob, Joshua and Emily, and wife, Julie, with all my heart; to the parents who encouraged my interest in nature and writing; and to our Father in Heaven for this glorious creation and the loved ones with whom we share its wonders.

ACKNOWLEDGEMENTS

Special thanks to the United States Fish and Wildlife Service, Dr. Hal Schramm and the Colorado Division of Wildlife, particularly Greg Gerlich, Doug Krieger and Kevin Rogers.

Cover and book design by Jonathan Norberg

Illustration credits by artist and page number:
  Cover illustrations: Greenback Cutthroat Trout (main) and Bluegill (upper) by Joseph Tomelleri
  Duane Raver/USFWS: 9 (both), 19, 22, 24, 26, 28, 30, 32, 36, 38, 42, 86, 94, 96 (top), 104, 122, 136, 138, 142, 144, 146, 148, 150, 152, 158, 160, 164 (inset) **MyFWC.com/fishing:** 10 **Joseph Tomelleri:** 34, 40, 44, 46 (all), 48, 50, 52, 54 (both), 56 (both), 58, 62 (both), 64, 66 (both), 68, 70 (all), 72 (both), 74, 76, 78, 80, 82 (both), 84, 90, 92, 96 (inset), 98, 100 (all), 102 (both), 106, 108 (all), 110, 112, 114 (both), 116, 118, 120 (both), 124, 126, 128, 130 (both), 132, 134, 140, 154, 156, 162, 164 (top) **Julie Martinez:** 60 **Timothy Knepp/USFWS:** 88

10 9 8 7 6

Fish of Colorado Field Guide: Cutthroats to catfish—your must-have resource

Copyright © 2007 by Dan Johnson
Published by Adventure Publications, an imprint of AdventureKEEN
310 Garfield Street South
Cambridge, Minnesota 55008
(800) 678-7006
www.adventurepublications.net

Printed in China
ISBN 978-1-59193-204-8 (pbk.), ISBN 978-1-59193-653-4 (ebook)

TABLE OF CONTENTS

Sunfish Family

Temperate Bass Family

Topminnow Family

HOW TO USE THIS BOOK

Your *Fish of Colorado Field Guide* is designed to make it easy to identify more than 80 species of the most common and important fish in Colorado, and learn fascinating facts about each species' range, natural history and more.

The fish are organized by families, such as Catfish (*Ictaluridae*), Perch (*Percidae*), Trout and Salmon (*Salmonidae*) and Sunfish (*Centrarchidae*), which are listed in alphabetical order. Within these families, individual species are arranged alphabetically in their appropriate groups. For example, members of the Sunfish family are divided into Black Bass, Crappie and True Sunfish groups. For a detailed list of fish families and individual species, turn to the Table of Contents (page 3); the Index (pp. 171-175) provides a handy reference guide to fish by common name (such as Lake Trout) and other common terms for the species.

Fish Identification

Determining a fish's body shape is the first step to identifying it. Each fish family usually exhibits one or sometimes two basic outlines. Catfish have long, stout bodies with flattened heads, barbels or "whiskers" around the mouth, a relatively tall but narrow dorsal fin and an adipose fin. There are two forms of Sunfish: the flat, round, plate-like outline we see in Bluegills; and the torpedo or "fusiform" shape of Largemouth Bass.

In this field guide you can quickly identify a fish by first matching its general body shape to one of the fish family silhouettes listed in the Table of Contents. From there, turn to that family's section and use the illustrations and text descriptions to identify your fish. A Sample Page (pg. 22) is provided to explain how the information is presented in each two-page spread.

For some species, the illustration will be enough to identify your catch, but it is important to note that your fish may not look exactly like the artwork. Fish frequently change colors. Males that are brightly colored during the spawning season may show muted coloration at other times. Likewise, bass caught in muddy streams show much less pattern than those taken from clear lakes—and all fish lose some of their markings and color when removed from the water.

Most fish are similar in appearance to one or more other species—often, but not always, within the same family. For example, the Black Crappie is remarkably similar to the White Crappie. To accurately identify such look-alikes, check the inset illustrations and accompanying notes below the main illustration, under the "Similar Species" heading.

Throughout *Fish of Colorado* we use basic biological and fisheries management terms that refer to physical characteristics or conditions of fish and their environment, such as "*dorsal*" fin or "*turbid*" water. For your convenience, these are listed and defined in the Glossary (pp. 166-170), along with other handy fish-related terms and their definitions.

Understanding such terminology will help you make sense of reports on state and federal research, fish population surveys, lake assessments, management plans and other important fisheries documents.

FISH ANATOMY

It's much easier to identify fish if you know the names of different parts of a fish. For example, it's easier to use the term "adipose fin" to indicate the small, soft, fleshy flap on a Rainbow Trout's back than try to describe it. The following illustrations point out the basic parts of a fish; the accompanying text defines these characteristics.

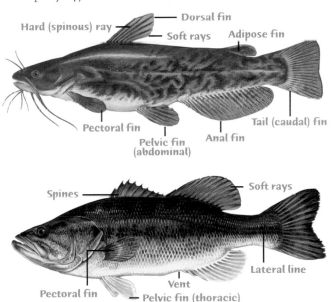

Fins are made up of bony structures that support a membrane. There are three kinds of bony structures in fins: **Soft rays** are flexible fin supports and are often branched.

Spines are stiff, often sharp supports that are not jointed. **Hard rays** are stiff, pointed, barbed structures that can be raised or lowered. Catfish are famous for their hard rays, which are often mistakenly called spines. Sunfish have soft rays associated with spines to form a prominent dorsal fin.

Fins are named by their position on the fish. The **dorsal fin** is on top along the midline. A few species have another fin on their back, called an **adipose fin**. This is small, fleshy protuberance located between the dorsal fin and the tail is distinctive of catfish, trout and salmon. **Pectoral fins** are found on each side of the fish near the gills. The **anal fin** is located along the midline, on the fish's bottom or *ventral* side. There is also a paired set of fins on the bottom of the fish, called the **pelvic fins**. These can be in the **thoracic position** (just below the pectoral fins) or farther back on the stomach, in the **abdominal position**. The tail is known as the **caudal fin**.

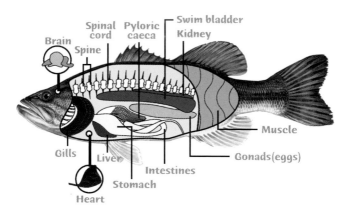

Eyes—A fish's eyes can detect color. Their eyes are rounder than those of mammals because of the refractive index of water; focus is achieved by moving the lens in and out, not distorting it as in mammals. Different species have varying levels of eyesight. Walleyes see well in low light. Bluegills have excellent daytime vision but see poorly at night, making them vulnerable to predation.

Nostrils—A pair of nostrils, or *nares*, are used to detect odors in the water. Eels and catfishes have particularly well-developed senses of smell.

Mouth—The shape of the mouth is a clue to what the fish eats. The larger the food it consumes, the larger the mouth.

Teeth—Not all fish have teeth, but those that do have mouthgear designed to help them feed. Walleyes, Northern Pike and Tiger Muskies have sharp *canine* teeth for grabbing and holding prey. Minnows have *pharyngeal* teeth—located in the throat—for grinding.

Catfish have *cardiform* teeth, which feel like a rough patch in the front of the mouth. Bass have patches of *vomerine* teeth on the roof of their mouth.

Swim Bladder—Almost all fish have a swim bladder, a balloon-like organ that helps the fish regulate its buoyancy.

Lateral Line—This sensory organ helps the fish detect movement in the water (to help avoid predators or capture prey) as well as water currents and pressure changes. It consists of fluid-filled sacs with hair-like sensors, which are open to the water through a row of pores in their skin along each side—creating a visible line along the fish's side.

FISH NAMES

A Walleye is a Walleye in Colorado. But in the northern parts of its range, Canadians call it a jack or jackfish. In the eastern U.S. it is often called a pickerel or walleyed pike.

Because common names may vary regionally, and even change for different sizes of the same species, scientific names are used that are exactly the same around the world. Each species has only one correct scientific name that can be recognized anywhere, in any language. The Walleye is *Sander vitreus* from Boulder to Berlin.

Scientific names are made up of Greek or Latin words that often describe the species. There are two parts to a scientific name: the generic or "genus," which is capitalized (*Sander*), and the specific name, which is not capitalized (*vitreus*). Both are displayed in italic text.

A species' genus represents a group of closely related fish. The Walleye and Sauger are in the same genus, so they share the generic name *Sander*. But each have different specific names, *vitreus* for Walleye, *canadense* for the Sauger.

ABOUT COLORADO FISH

The Centennial State is rich in aquatic diversity. Habitats range from gin-clear, high-elevation streams and lakes to warm, cloudy, fertile plains reservoirs. With over 50,000 miles of streams and more than 4,000 natural lakes and man-made impoundments, Colorado offers a profusion of opportunities to watch, study and pursue fish.

FREQUENTLY ASKED QUESTIONS

What is a fish?

Fish are aquatic, typically cold-blooded animals that have backbones, gills and fins.

Are all fish cold-blooded?

All freshwater fish are cold-blooded. Recently it has been discovered that some members of the saltwater Tuna family are warm-blooded. Whales and Bottlenose Dolphins are also warm-blooded, but they are mammals, not fish.

Do all fish have scales?

No. Most fish have scales that look like those on the Common Goldfish. A few, such as Alligator Gar, have scales that resemble armor plates. Catfish have no scales at all.

How do fish breathe?

A fish takes in water through its mouth and forces it through its gills, where a system of fine membranes absorbs oxygen from the water, and releases carbon dioxide. Gills cannot pump air efficiently over these membranes, which quickly dry out and stick together. Fish should never be out of the water longer than you can hold your breath.

Can fish breathe air?

Some species can; gars have a modified swim bladder that acts like a lung. Fish that can't breathe air may die when dissolved oxygen in the water falls below critical levels.

How do fish swim?

Fish swim by contracting bands of muscles on alternate sides of their body so the tail is whipped rapidly from side to side. Pectoral and pelvic fins are used mainly for stability when a fish hovers, but are sometimes used during rapid bursts of forward motion.

Do all fish look like fish?

Most do and are easily recognizable as fish. The eels and lampreys are fish, but they look like snakes. Sculpins look like little goblins with bat wings.

Where can you find fish?

Some fish species can be found in almost any body of water, but not all fish are found everywhere. Each is designed to exploit a particular habitat. The Arkansas Darter is found in clear, shallow spring-fed creeks, while the Colorado Pikeminnow prefers large rivers.

A species may move around within its home water, sometimes migrating hundreds of miles between lakes, rivers and tributary streams. Some movements, such as spawning migrations, are seasonal and very predictable.

Fish may also move horizontally from one area to another, or vertically in the water column, in response to changes in environmental conditions and food availability. In addition, many fish have daily travel patterns. By studying a species' habitat, food and spawning information in this book—and understanding how it interacts with other Colorado fish—it is possible to make an educated prediction of where to find it in any lake, stream or river.

WHIRLING DISEASE

Whirling disease affects trout and salmon. It is thought to be a major factor in the decline of wild Rainbow Trout in some Colorado waters. It is caused by a microscopic parasite (*Myxobolus cerebralis*) that attacks soft cartilage, causing nerve damage, skeletal deformities and sometimes death. The disease likely originated in Europe, where native Brown Trout are resistant to the parasite.

Whirling disease has been confirmed in 13 of Colorado's 15 major drainages, including the Colorado, South Platte, Gunnison, Arkansas and Rio Grande rivers. There is no practical cure to treat infected wild trout, but the Colorado Division of Wildlife has developed policies and regulations to help control and prevent its spread.

You Can Help

—Wash off any mud from vehicles, boats, trailers, anchors, axles, waders, boots, fishing equipment and anything that can hold the spores or mud-dwelling worms.

—Drain boats, equipment, coolers, live bait wells and any holder of water.

—Don't transport fish from one body of water to another. This can help spread whirling disease. It is unlawful in Colorado to move and stock live fish without a license.

—Don't dispose of fish entrails or other by-products into any body of water.

—Never transport aquatic plants. Make sure boats, props, anchors and trailers are cleared of weeds after every use.

INVASIVE SPECIES

While many introduced species have great recreational value, such as Rainbow Trout, Lake Trout and Brown Trout, many exotic species have caused problems. Never move fish, water or vegetation from one lake or stream to another, and always follow state laws. For details, visit the Division of Wildlife website, http://wildlife.state.co.us.

FUN WITH FISH

There are many ways to enjoy Colorado's fish, from reading about them in this book to watching them in the wild. You can don a dive mask and jump in, wear polarized glasses to observe them from above the surface, or use an underwater camera (or sonar) to monitor fish behavior year-round.

Hands-on activities are also popular. Nearly 1 million resident and nonresident anglers enjoy pursuing Colorado's game fish. The sport offers a great chance to enjoy the outdoors with friends and family, and in many cases, bring home a healthy meal of fresh fish at the end of the day.

Proceeds from license sales, along with special taxes anglers pay on fishing supplies and motorboat fuel, fund the majority of fish management efforts, including fish surveys, the development of special regulations and stocking programs. The sport also has a huge impact on Colorado's economy, supporting thousands of jobs in fishing, tourism and related industries.

OPPORTUNITIES FOR NONRESIDENTS

More than 200,000 nonresidents sample Colorado's remarkable fisheries each year. A wealth of resources are available to help out-of-state anglers (as well as residents) enjoy the full bounty of opportunities.

One source is the Division of Wildlife (DOW) website: http://wildlife.state.co.us. Helpful information is also available at the following numbers:

General fishing season dates and license fees.
(303) 291-7533

Fish stocking: (303) 291-7531

Fishing conditions reports (available April through August):

Statewide: (303) 291-7534

Metro Denver and Foothills: (303) 291-7535

Northeastern Colorado: (303) 291-7536

Northwestern Colorado: (303) 291-7537

Southeastern Colorado: (303) 291-7538

Southwestern Colorado: (303) 291-7539

In addition, outfitters, guides, fly shops and bait dealers are great resources. So are reputable fishing organizations such as the Colorado Walleye Association (719-481-4647; www.cwaonline.net) and local chapters of the Colorado B.A.S.S. Federation (www.coloradobassfederation.org) and Trout Unlimited (www.tu.org).

CATCH-AND-RELEASE FISHING

Selective harvest (keeping some fish to eat and releasing the rest) and total catch-and-release fishing allow anglers to enjoy the sport without harming the resource. Catch-and-release is especially important with certain species and sizes of fish, and in lakes or rivers where biologists are trying to improve the fishery by protecting large predators or breeding age, adult fish. The fishing regulations, DOW website and your local fisheries office are excellent sources of advice on which fish to keep and which to release.

Catch-and-release is only truly successful if the fish survives the experience. Following are helpful tips to help reduce the chances of post-release mortality.

- Play and land fish quickly.

- Wet your hands before touching a fish, to avoid removing its protective slime coating.

- Handle the fish gently and keep it in the water if possible.

- Do not hold the fish by the eye sockets or gills. Hold it horizontally and support its belly.

- If a fish is deeply hooked, cut the line so at least an inch hangs outside the mouth. This helps the hook lie flush when the fish takes in food.

- Circle hooks may help reduce deeply hooked fish.

- Don't fish deep water unless you plan to keep your catch.

- Don't release fish kept on a stringer or in a livewell. In Colorado, these fish count in your limit.

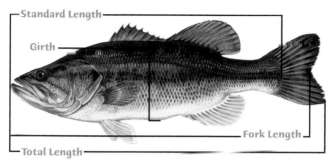

Standard Length

Girth

Fork Length

Total Length

FISH MEASUREMENT

Fish are measured in three ways: standard length, fork length and total length. The first two are more accurate, because tails are often damaged or worn down. Total length is used in slot limits.

The following formulas estimate the weight of popular game fish. Lengths are in inches; weight is in pounds.

Formulas

Bass weight = (length x length x girth) / 1,200
Pike weight = (length x length x length) / 3,500
Sunfish weight = (length x length x length) / 1,200
Trout weight = (length x girth x girth) / 800
Walleye weight = (length x length x length) / 2,700

For example, let's say that you catch a 16-inch Walleye. Using the formula for Walleyes above: (16 x 16 x 16) divided by 2,700 = 1.5 pounds. Your Walleye would weigh approximately 1.5 pounds.

COLORADO STATE RECORD FISH

SPECIES	WEIGHT (LBS.-OZ.)	WHERE CAUGHT	YEAR
Arctic Char	3-12	Dillon Reservoir	1994
Bass, Largemouth	11-6	Echo Canyon Reservoir	1997
Bass, Striped	12-13	CF & I Reservoir No. 2	1984
Bass, Smallmouth	5-12	Navajo Reservoir	1993
Bass, White	4-7	Blue Lake	1963
Bass, Rock	1-1.25	Ramah Reservoir	1979
Bass, Spotted	4-7.825	Valco Ponds	2005
Bluegill	2-4	Hollenbeck Reservoir	1988
Bullhead, Black	5-1	Farm Pond	1993
Carp	35-5	Glenmere Park	2001
Carp, Grass	44-8	Private Lake	2006
Catfish, Blue	20-1	Private Lake	1976
Catfish, Channel	33-8	Hertha Reservoir	1994
Catfish, Flathead	3-2.75	Pueblo Reservoir	2005
Crappie, Black	3-4	Private Pond	1990
Crappie, White	4-3.75	Northglenn Lake	1975
Drum, Freshwater	17-3	Lonetree Reservoir	1978
Eel, American	3-1	Flagler Reservoir	1996
Grayling	1-10	Lower Big Creek Lake	2002
Muskellunge, Tiger	40-2	Quincy Reservoir	1994
Perch, Sacramento	1-14	Banner Lakes	1974
Perch, Yellow	2-5	Gravel Pit	1983
Pike, Northern	30-11	Stagecoach Reservoir	2006
Salmon, Chinook	11-0	Williams Fork Reservoir	1989
Salmon, Kokanee (Angling)	6-13	Spinney Mountain Reservoir	1986
Salmon, Kokanee (Snagging)	7-5	Blue Mesa Reservoir	2002
Sauger	3-1	CF & I Reservoir No. 3	1980
Saugeye	10-14	John Martin Reservoir	2001
Sucker (Flannelmouth)	4-5.5	Colorado River	1990
Sunfish, Green (tie)	1-5	Big Thompson Pond, Gravel Pit	1997, 2001
Sunfish, Hybrid	1-8.5	Gravel Pit	1986
Sunfish, Bluegill	2-4	Hollenbeck Reservoir	1988
Tench	5-6	Home Lake	1998

SPECIES	WEIGHT (LBS.-OZ.)	WHERE CAUGHT	YEAR
Trout, Brook	7-10	Upper Cataract Lake	1947
Trout, Brown	30-8	Roaring Judy Ponds	1988
Trout, Cutthroat (Native)	16-0	Twin Lakes	1964
Trout, Cutthroat (Snake River)	17-2.6	Blue River	2005
Trout, Lake	46-14.6	Blue Mesa Reservoir	2003
Trout, Rainbow	19-10	Morrow Point Reservoir	2003
Trout, Splake	18-15	Island Lake	1976
Trout, Tiger	4-15	Private Pond	2005
Trout, Golden	3-12	Kelly Lake	1979
Walleye	18-13	Standley Lake	1997
Wiper	26-15	Pueblo Reservoir	2004
Whitefish	5-2	Roaring Fork River	1982

FISH CONSUMPTION ADVISORIES

Most fish are safe for us to eat. They are also a healthy source of low-fat protein. But because most of the world's surface water contains some industrial contaminants, and Colorado's lakes and rivers are no exception, any store-bought or sport-caught fish could contain mercury, PCBs or other contaminants.

The state Department of Public Health and Environment has issued detailed information on eating fish, including advisories on fish consumption for sport-caught species. Call (303) 692-3550 or visit www.cdphe.state.co.us (look under Environment A-Z, then go to F) for details.

Description: brief summary of physical characteristics to help you identify the fish, such as coloration and markings, body shape, fin size and placement

Similar Species: list of other fish that look similar and the pages on which they can be found; includes detailed inset drawings (below) highlighting key physical traits such as markings, mouth size or shape and fin characteristics to help you distinguish this fish from similar species

Rainbow Trout	**Brown Trout**	**Rainbow Trout**	**Brook Trout**
pinkish stripe on silvery body	sides lack pinkish stripe	lacks wormlike markings	wormlike marks on back

COMMON NAME

Scientific Name

Other Names: common terms or nicknames you may hear to describe this species

Habitat: environment where the fish is found (such as streams, rivers, small or large lakes, fast-flowing or still water, in or around vegetation, near shore, in clear water)

Range: geographic distribution, starting with the fish's overall range, followed by state-specific information

Food: what the fish eats most of the time (such as crustaceans, insects, fish, plankton)

Reproduction: timing of and behavior during the spawning period (such as dates and water temperatures, migration information, preferred spawning habitat, type of nest if applicable, colonial or solitary nester, parental care for eggs or fry)

Average Size: average length or range of length, average weight or range of weight

Records: state—the state record for this species, location and year; North American—the North American record for this species, location and year (from the National Fresh Water Fishing Hall of Fame)

Notes: interesting natural history information; this can be unique behaviors, remarkable features, sporting and table quality, or details on annual migrations, seasonal patterns or population trends

Description: back black to olive; sides yellowish green; belly cream to yellow; light bar on base of tail; barbels (dark at base) around mouth; adipose fin; scaleless skin; rounded tail

Similar Species: Brown Bullhead (pg. 26), Flathead Catfish (pg. 32), Stonecat (pg. 34)

Black Bullhead	**Stonecat**	**Black Bullhead**	**Flathead Catfish**
free adipose fin	fused adipose fin	slight overbite	pronounced underbite

Black Bullhead	**Brown Bullhead**
olive back and sides	mottled back and sides

BLACK BULLHEAD

Ameiurus melas

Other Names: common bullhead, horned pout

Habitat: shallow, slow-moving streams and backwaters; lakes and ponds—tolerates extremely turbid (cloudy) conditions

Range: southern Canada through the Great Lakes and the Mississippi River watershed into Mexico and the Southwest; native to eastern Colorado, introduced statewide

Food: a scavenging opportunist, feeds mostly on animal material (live or dead) but will eat plant matter

Reproduction: spawns from late April to early June; excavates nest in shallow water with a muddy bottom; both sexes guard nest and eggs, which hatch in 4 to 6 days; adults guard the fry until they are about 1 inch in length

Average Size: 8 to 10 inches, 4 to 16 ounces

Records: state—5 pounds, 1 ounce, Farm Pond, 1993; North American—8 pounds, 15 ounces, Sturgis Pond, Michigan, 1987

Notes: One of Colorado's most abundant warmwater species, the Black Bullhead tolerates silt, pollution, low oxygen levels and tepid water temperatures better than most fish. It is often found with other hardy species such as the Fathead Minnow and Green Sunfish. The Black Bullhead feeds mainly on the bottom. Adults typically rest in deep water during the day, then move shallower as darkness falls to scavenge until shortly before daybreak. Fry school in tight swarms along shorelines throughout their first summer.

Description: yellowish brown upper body, with mottling on back and sides; barbels around mouth; adipose fin; scaleless skin; rounded tail; well-defined barbs on the pectoral spines

Similar Species: Black Bullhead (pg. 24), Flathead Catfish (pg. 32), Stonecat (pg. 34)

Brown Bullhead	Stonecat		Brown Bullhead	Flathead Catfish
free adipose fin	fused adipose fin		slight overbite	pronounced underbite

Brown Bullhead	Black Bullhead
mottled back and sides	olive back and sides

BROWN BULLHEAD
Ameiurus nebulosus

Other Names: marbled or speckled bullhead, creek or red cat

Habitat: warm, weedy lakes and sluggish streams

Range: southern Canada through the Great Lakes to Florida, introduced in the West; in Colorado, introduced in the South Platte drainage and potentially other locations

Food: a scavenging opportunist; feeds mostly on insects, fish, fish eggs, snails and leeches but will eat plant matter

Reproduction: in early summer female and male build nest in shallow water with a sand or rocky bottom, often in cover offering shade; both sexes guard eggs and young

Average Size: 7 to 15 inches, 4 ounces to 2 pounds

Records: state—none; North American—6 pounds, 2 ounces, Pearl River, Mississippi, 1991

Notes: A highly adaptable member of the Catfish clan, the Brown Bullhead thrives in a variety of habitats, from river backwaters to deep, clear lakes. It tolerates low oxygen levels and very turbid (cloudy) water, but prefers clean, clear, weedy lakes with soft bottoms. Though it favors water temperatures ranging from 78 to 82 degrees, it can survive warmer conditions. Primarily a bottom feeder, the Brown Bullhead is most active at night, when it uses its sensitive barbels and other senses to home in on a wide variety of prey. Not highly pursued by anglers, though it is easy to catch on worms, minnows or prepared baits, and its reddish meat is fine table fare.

Description: pale bluish-silver to slate-gray back and sides (similar to channel catfish but lacks spots on back and sides); light underside; forked tail

Similar Species: Channel Catfish (pg. 30)

Blue Catfish

anal fin straight, with 30 or more rays

Channel Catfish

anal fin curved, with 24 to 29 rays

BLUE CATFISH

Ictalurus furcatus

Other Names: blue fulton, chucklehead, silver or white cat

Habitat: large rivers and reservoirs; prefers strong current and silt-free bottom such as sand, gravel or small rocks

Range: native to the Mississippi River basin and Gulf Slope drainages from Alabama to New Mexico; introduced in the Arkansas, upper Rio Grande and Platte systems in Colorado

Food: fish, insects, crayfish, mussels

Reproduction: matures at about 24 inches in length; spawns April through June when water temperatures reach 70 to 75 degrees; male fans out nest in cavity such as a hole in the bank; female deposits egg mass, which male guards

Average Size: 20 to 44 inches, 3 to 40 pounds

Records: state—20 pounds, 1 ounce, Private Lake, 1976; North American—124 pounds, Mississippi R., Illinois, 2005

Notes: Thanks to its large size, fighting power and fine flavor, the Blue Catfish is a favorite of anglers. It is a big-water species found in the main channels and major tributaries of large rivers, as well as reservoirs. Within a given system, it is migratory—often in response to water temperature (the preferred range is 77 to 82 degrees). Anglers often target blues by looking for the large predators shadowing schools of baitfish such as Gizzard Shad, then dropping live fish or cutbait to the level of the catfish. Although the all-tackle record is just over 120 pounds, giant Blue Catfish weighing more than 200 pounds were reported prior to 1900.

Description: gray to silver back and sides; white belly; black spots on sides; large fish lack spots and appear dark olive or slate; forked tail; adipose fin; long barbels around mouth

Similar Species: Blue Catfish (pg. 28), Flathead Catfish (pg. 32), Bullheads (pp. 24-27)

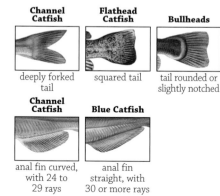

Channel Catfish	**Flathead Catfish**	**Bullheads**
deeply forked tail	squared tail	tail rounded or slightly notched

Channel Catfish	**Blue Catfish**
anal fin curved, with 24 to 29 rays	anal fin straight, with 30 or more rays

CHANNEL CATFISH
Ictalurus punctatus

Other Names: spotted, speckled or silver catfish, fiddler

Habitat: medium to large streams with deep pools, low to moderate current and sand, gravel or rubble bottom; also found in warm lakes; tolerates turbid (cloudy) conditions

Range: southern Canada through the Midwest into Mexico and Florida; widely introduced; native to eastern Colorado, introduced in warmwater rivers and reservoirs statewide

Food: insects, crustaceans, fish, some plant matter

Reproduction: matures at 5 to 8 years; in summer when water temperature reaches about 70 to 85 degrees, male builds nest in dark, sheltered area, such as undercut bank; female deposits 2,000 to 21,000 eggs, which hatch in 6 to 10 days; male guards eggs and young until the nest is deserted

Average Size: 12 to 20 inches, 3 to 4 pounds

Records: state—33 pounds, 8 ounces, Hertha Reservoir, 1994; North American—58 pounds, Santee Cooper Reservoir, South Carolina, 1964

Notes: The Channel Catfish is a strong fighter that hits a variety of prepared baits from doughballs to stinkbaits. Its white, sweet fillets are excellent table fare. Often holds in deep water or cover by day, then moves into riffles or other shallow feeding areas at night. Primarily uses taste buds in its barbels and skin to locate food. However, its relatively large eyes also allow it to feed by sight. Typically a bottom feeder, it will suspend or rise to the surface on occasion.

31

Description: color variable, usually mottled yellow or brown; belly cream to yellow; adipose fin; chin barbels; lacks scales; head broad and flat; tail squared; pronounced underbite

Similar Species: Bullheads (pp. 24-27), Channel Catfish (pg. 30), Stonecat (pg. 34)

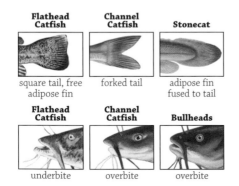

Flathead Catfish	Channel Catfish	Stonecat
square tail, free adipose fin	forked tail	adipose fin fused to tail

Flathead Catfish	Channel Catfish	Bullheads
underbite	overbite	overbite

FLATHEAD CATFISH

Pylodictis olivaris

Other Names: shovel-nose, shovelhead, yellow cat, mud cat, pied cat, Mississippi cat

Habitat: deep pools of large rivers and impoundments

Range: the Mississippi River watershed and into Mexico; large rivers in the Southwest; introduced into the Arkansas and Platte rivers in Colorado

Food: fish, crayfish

Reproduction: matures at age 4 to 5, when it is about 18 inches in length; spawns when water is 72 to 80 degrees; male builds and defends nest in hollow log, undercut bank or other secluded area; female may lay more than 30,000 eggs, depending on her size and condition; male guards young to about 7 days after hatching

Average Size: 15 to 45 inches; 1 to 45 pounds

Records: state—3 pounds, 2.75 ounces, Pueblo Reservoir, 2005; North American—123 pounds, Elk River Reservoir, Kansas, 1998

Notes: This large, typically solitary predator is a strong fighter with firm, white flesh. It feeds aggressively on live fish, often at night, when it moves from deep water in pools (or cover, such as a logjam) into riffles and shallow areas of pools. Unlike the Channel Catfish, it is not a scavenger and rarely eats decaying animal matter. Has been used to control stunted panfish and bullheads; in some waters it is blamed for reducing native fish populations.

Description: dark olive to brown; large, fleshy head; protruding upper jaw; adipose fin continuous with tail

Similar Species: Bullheads (pp. 24-27), Catfish (pp. 28-33)

Stonecat	Bullheads	Catfish
fused adipose fin	free adipose fin	free adipose fin

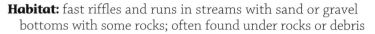

STONECAT
Noturus flavus

Other Name: willow cat

Habitat: fast riffles and runs in streams with sand or gravel bottoms with some rocks; often found under rocks or debris

Range: St. Lawrence, Great Lakes, Hudson Bay (Red River) and Mississippi River basins from Quebec to Alberta, south to northern Alabama, northern Mississippi and northeast Oklahoma; native to Colorado's eastern plains, found in the Republican and South Platte basins

Food: small invertebrates, algae and other plant matter

Reproduction: matures in 3 to 9 years; spawns in late spring and early summer; not nest builders; female lays tight cluster of eggs under objects such as roots, rocks and logs or in abandoned crayfish burrows; male guards the eggs

Average Size: up to 12 inches

Records: none

Notes: This small, secretive fish is only active at night. It has poison glands at the base of the dorsal and pectoral fins. Though not lethal, the toxin produces a painful burning sensation, reputed to bring even the hardiest humans to their knees, if only for a short time. Though it is a species of special concern in Colorado, the Stonecat is common in other parts of its range and is commonly used as bait by Walleye anglers in some states.

Description: humped back, dorsal fin extends from hump to near tail; back is gray with purple or bronze reflections, silver sides, white underbelly; lateral line extends from the head through the tail

Similar Species: Wiper (pg. 162)

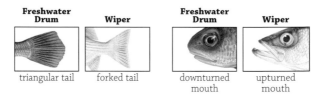

Freshwater Drum	Wiper	Freshwater Drum	Wiper
triangular tail	forked tail	downturned mouth	upturned mouth

FRESHWATER DRUM

Aplodinotus grunniens

Other Names: sheepshead, croaker, thunderpumper, grinder

Habitat: slow- to moderate-current areas of large streams and rivers; shallow lakes, often with mud or sand bottoms; tolerates turbid (cloudy) water

Range: Canada south through Midwest into eastern Mexico to Guatemala; introduced in the Republican, Arkansas and Platte drainages of eastern Colorado

Food: small fish, insects, crayfish, clams

Reproduction: in May and June after water temperature reaches about 66 degrees, schools of drum randomly lay eggs in open water near surface, over sand or gravel; no nest or parental care

Average Size: 12 to 20 inches, 12 ounces to 5 pounds

Records: state—17 pounds, 3 ounces, Lonetree Reservoir, 1978; North American—54 pounds, 8 ounces, Nickajack Lake, Tennessee, 1972

Notes: Only member of the drum family found strictly in freshwater. Named for grunting noise produced by males, primarily to attract females. The sound is produced by muscles rubbed along the swim bladder. The Freshwater Drum was stocked in Colorado in the early 1950s as a sportfish. Now unpopular with anglers, it is occasionally caught while trolling for other species; it can also be taken on live bait fished on the bottom. Its flaky white flesh is tasty but easily dries out due to its low oil content.

Description: long, snake-like body; large mouth; pectoral fins, gill slits and continuous dorsal, tail and anal fin; dark brown on top with yellow sides and white belly

Similar Species: none

AMERICAN EEL
Anguilla rostrata

Other Names: common or freshwater eel

Habitat: soft bottoms of medium to large streams

Range: Atlantic Ocean, eastern and central North America and eastern Central America; rare in Colorado, reported from the San Luis Valley, Conejos County, where eels escaped from an aquaculture facility; the state record was caught in Flagler Reservoir

Food: insects, crayfish, small fish, frogs

Reproduction: a "catadromous" species, it spends most of its life in freshwater and spawns in the mid–North Atlantic Ocean in the Sargasso Sea; female may lay up to 20 million eggs; adults die after spawning

Average Size: 24 to 36 inches

Records: state—3 pounds, 1 ounce, Flagler Reservoir, 1996; North American—8 pounds, 8 ounces, Cliff Pond, Massachusetts, 1992

Notes: Leaf-shaped larval eels drift with ocean currents for about a year. When they reach river mouths of North and Central America, they develop into small eels (elvers). Males remain in estuaries; females migrate far upstream, reportedly crawling along shore or over concrete dams when possible to bypass obstructions. At maturity (up to 20 years of age) adults return to the Sargasso Sea. Rarely seen, the American Eel is most active at night, often resting under rocks, sunken logs and other cover during the day.

Description: deep body; silvery blue back with white sides and belly; small mouth; last rays of dorsal fin form a long thread; younger fish have a dark spot behind the gill flap

Similar Species: Freshwater Drum (pg. 36)

Gizzard Shad	Freshwater Drum
forked tail	triangular tail

GIZZARD SHAD
Dorosoma cepedianum

Other Names: hickory or jack shad, skipjack

Habitat: quiet water of large rivers, reservoirs, lakes, swamps; brackish and saline waters in coastal areas

Range: St. Lawrence River and Great Lakes, Mississippi, Atlantic and Gulf Slope drainages from Quebec to Mexico, south to central Florida; in Colorado, found in the Arkansas, South Platte and Republican drainages

Food: algae, zooplankton, insect larvae

Reproduction: spawns May through June in tributary streams and sheltered bays; mixed schools of males and females roil at the surface, releasing eggs and milt without regard for individual mates; the adhesive eggs sink to bottom and hatch in 2 to 7 days

Average Size: 6 to 14 inches, 1 to 16 ounces

Records: North American—4 pounds, 12 ounces, Lake Oahe, South Dakota, 2006

Notes: The prolific Gizzard Shad is an important food source for predators. Found in a variety of Colorado waters, it does best in fertile reservoirs. Look for large schools at or near the surface in areas lacking current, or with a slight flow. The name "gizzard" refers to its long, convoluted intestine, which may be packed with sand. Filters plankton, algae and suspended organic matter through its gill rakers and "grazes" the bottom for insects and organic sediment. Large shad may be caught with hook and line but have little food value.

Description: two pairs of barbels near round, extendable mouth; brassy yellow to golden brown or dark-olive sides; white belly; some red on tail and anal fin; each scale has a dark spot at the base and a dark margin

Similar Species: Grass Carp (pg. 44), River Carpsucker (pg. 122)

Common Carp	**Grass Carp**	**River Carpsucker**
down-turned mouth with barbels	forward facing mouth lacks barbels	mouth lacks barbels

COMMON CARP

Cyprinus carpio

Other Names: German or leather carp, buglemouth

Habitat: warm, shallow, quiet, well-vegetated waters of both streams and lakes

Range: native to Asia, widely introduced; in Colorado, most warmwater lakes and rivers, some coldwater lakes

Food: prefers insects, crustaceans and mollusks but at times eats algae and other plants, even small fish

Reproduction: spawns from late spring to early summer in very shallow water at stream and lake edges; spawning adults are easily seen due to energetic splashing along shore

Average Size: 16 to 18 inches, 5 to 20 pounds

Records: state—35 pounds, 5 ounces, Glenmere Park, 2001; North American—57 pounds, 13 ounces, Tidal Basin, Washington D.C., 1983

Notes: A fast-growing Asian minnow, it was introduced in North America as a food fish but is now considered a pest. It is very prolific and often uproots aquatic plants and increases turbidity in shallow lakes, causing a decline in waterfowl and native fish populations that require clean water. The Common Carp arrived in Colorado in 1879 and is currently found in most warmwater lakes and rivers, and even some coldwater lakes such as Elevenmile Reservoir. Not popular with most Colorado anglers, but some fish for it with nymphs, streamers and natural baits.

Description: gold to olive or silver back fading to yellowish-white underside; broad, blunt head; forward-facing mouth; thick body; large, dark-edged scales; low-set eyes

Similar Species: Common Carp (pg. 42)

Grass Carp

forward facing mouth lacks barbels

Common Carp

down-turned mouth with barbels

GRASS CARP

Ctenopharyngodon idella

Cyprinidae

Other Names: white amur

Habitat: quiet waters of lakes, ponds, pools and backwaters of large rivers

Range: native to eastern Asia from Amur River of eastern Russia and China to the West River in southern China and Thailand; widely introduced in North America; released into some Colorado waters for vegetation control

Food: aquatic vegetation including filamentous algae

Reproduction: spawns in main channel areas from late spring to early summer when water temperatures reach 53 to 63 degrees; eggs drift with the current and must remain suspended during incubation, which lasts 20 to 40 hours; for this reason long stretches of flowing water are required

Average Size: 16 to 40 inches, 5 to 50 pounds

Records: state—44 pounds, 8 ounces, Private Lake, 2006; North American—78 pounds, 12 ounces, Flint River, Georgia, 2003

Notes: The Grass Carp is an herbivore (plant eater) with a voracious appetite, known to consume from 40 to 300 percent of its body weight each day. It is also one of the largest members of the Minnow family, reportedly reaching lengths of 48 inches and weights well over 100 pounds in its native range. It has been stocked in North America as a food fish and to control aquatic vegetation. Because it eats plants, it is rarely caught on hook and line.

CREEK CHUB

RIO GRANDE CHUB

SUCKERMOUTH MINNOW

Description: dark olive back; iridescent purple or silver sides; white belly; dark spot at base of dorsal fin

Similar Species: Hornyhead Chub (pg. 50), Rio Grande Chub, Suckermouth Minnow

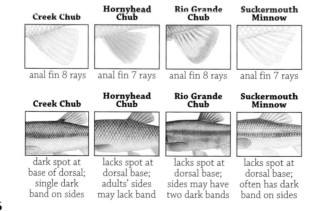

Creek Chub	Hornyhead Chub	Rio Grande Chub	Suckermouth Minnow
anal fin 8 rays	anal fin 7 rays	anal fin 8 rays	anal fin 7 rays

Creek Chub	Hornyhead Chub	Rio Grande Chub	Suckermouth Minnow
dark spot at base of dorsal; single dark band on sides	lacks spot at dorsal base; adults' sides may lack band	lacks spot at dorsal base; sides may have two dark bands	lacks spot at dorsal base; often has dark band on sides

CREEK CHUB

Semotilus atromaculatus

Cyprinidae

Other Names: brook or common chub, horned dace

Habitat: small to medium-size streams and rivers with gravel, sand or rubble bottom; tolerates turbid (cloudy) conditions but prefers clear water

Range: eastern U.S. and southeastern Canada from Manitoba south through Colorado and eastern Texas; in Colorado, the Arkansas, Republican and South Platte basins; also found in the Yampa River and tributaries of the Colorado River

Food: insects, small fish, fish eggs, crayfish, worms, mollusks

Reproduction: spawns in spring at water temperatures of 55 to 65 degrees; male builds and guards nest in gravel above or below a riffle, or at the lower end of a pool in moderate current; when complete, the nest is a short ridge of stones with a shallow pit on the downstream end; female deposits 25 to 50 eggs at a time; male covers fertilized eggs

Average Size: 7 to 12 inches, 8 to 12 ounces

Records: none

Notes: The Creek Chub is a food source for many predators. Large adults are solitary, often hiding beneath undercut banks or root wads; small chubs school with other minnows. The male defends its nest by using breeding tubercles on its head to strike intruders. Related to the similar Rio Grande Chub (*Gila pandora*) of the Rio Grande and Colorado basins; and Suckermouth Minnow (*Phenacobius mirabilis*), found in the Arkansas and South Platte basins.

47

Description: tan to brown back; silver sides; flattened snout overhangs large mouth; barbel at corner of mouth; broad, wedge-shaped head

Similar Species: Hornyhead Chub, (pg. 50)

Flathead Chub

pectoral fins extend almost to base of dorsal

Hornyhead Chub

pectoral fins barely halfway to dorsal base

FLATHEAD CHUB

Cyprinidae

Platygobio gracilis

Other Names: none

Habitat: main branches of turbid (cloudy) streams and rivers; often found in fast current with sand or gravel bottom; also occurs in the pools of small, clear streams

Range: Mackenzie, Saskatchewan and Lake Winnipeg drainages in Canada south through the plains states bordering the Rocky Mountains to New Mexico and Arkansas; in Colorado, the Arkansas River basin

Food: terrestrial and aquatic invertebrates, algae

Reproduction: matures at 2 years; spawns in summer; little is known about its spawning behavior

Average Size: 4 to 9 inches

Records: none

Notes: The Flathead Chub ranges from the Yukon to New Mexico, giving it among the largest north-south distributions in the Cyprinidae family. Studies indicate the Flathead Chub relies heavily on external taste buds to locate food, and it may be outcompeted by sight feeders such as various shiners. This may help explain its fondness for cloudy water conditions. It is an active fish, often moving in mixed schools with other species of minnows.

Description: gray to olive brown, often with a dark stripe on side and black spot at the base of tail; red spot behind eye; breeding males develop hornlike tubercles on the head

Similar Species: Creek Chub (pg. 46), Fathead Minnow (pg. 66), Suckermouth Minnow (pg. 46)

Hornyhead Chub	Creek Chub	Fathead Minnow	Suckermouth Minnow
down-turned mouth barely extends to front of eye	large mouth extends almost to middle of eye	upturned mouth does not extend to eye	sucker-shaped mouth does not extend to eye

HORNYHEAD CHUB

Cyprinidae

Nocomis biguttatus

Other Names: redtail, horned or river chub

Habitat: small to medium-size streams; occasionally found in lakes near stream mouths

Range: northern Midwest through the Great Lakes region; isolated populations in Cheyenne and Platte drainages of Wyoming and Colorado

Food: small aquatic invertebrates, zooplankton, algae and other plant matter, small fish

Reproduction: matures at 2 to 3 years; in late spring male excavates a 1- to 3-foot-diameter pit in gravelly stream riffle, then fills it with small stones (carried by mouth), creating a 6- to 8-inch-high mound; females lay eggs on the mound; male covers fertilized eggs with gravel; other species such as Common Shiner may use the mound for spawning; some research suggests the two males cooperate to defend it

Average Size: 4 to 12 inches

Records: none

Notes: A fish of clear-water streams with permanent flows and predominantly hard bottoms, the Hornyhead may be affected by siltation and the reduction of stream flows due to agriculture. Adults commonly hold in riffles but avoid the swiftest currents, forming loose, mixed schools with shiners and other minnows. Predominantly a sight feeder. Where common it is often used as bait by anglers, who often refer to it as a Redtail Chub.

Description: distinguished by pronounced hump behind the head; greenish back fading to silver sides; white belly; snout overhangs lip

Similar Species: Razorback Sucker (pg. 132)

Humpback Chub	**Razorback Sucker**	**Humpback Chub**	**Razorback Sucker**
pronounced hump behind head	ridge behind head lacks pronounced hump	9 rays in dorsal fin	13 to 16 rays in dorsal fin

HUMPBACK CHUB
Gila cypha

Other Names: none

Habitat: pools and eddies in areas of fast-flowing, deep, turbid (cloudy) water, often associated with cliffs and boulders

Range: historically found throughout the Colorado River system from the Green River in Wyoming to the Gulf of California; in Colorado, the Green, Gunnison, Yampa and Colorado rivers

Food: small insects, algae

Reproduction: spawns April through July during high water from snowmelt

Average Size: 12 to 16 inches, 12 ounces to 2 pounds

Records: none

Notes: A remarkable and striking member of the minnow family, the Humpback Chub is a state and federally listed endangered species. Once common throughout the Colorado River system, its populations declined due to dam construction and water diversion projects, which lower water temperatures and block migrations. Restoration efforts include the removal of non-native fish. Though it inhabits whitewater canyons, it lacks the speed and strength of the Colorado Pikeminnow. Rather, it relies on its large fins to glide through slow-water areas as it feeds on insects.

Description: olive to brown or black back, fading to white or yellowish underneath; may have dark blotches on sides, and dark stripe ahead of eye; upper jaw and snout extend well beyond lower jaw; small barbel in corner of mouth; breeding males develop reddish orange on head and fins

Similar Species: Northern Redbelly Dace (pg. 56), Southern Redbelly Dace (pg. 56)

Longnose Dace	**Northern Redbelly Dace**	**Southern Redbelly Dace**
upper jaw and snout extend well beyond lower jaw	curved mouth, lower jaw slightly ahead of upper	straight mouth, upper jaw slightly ahead of lower jaw

LONGNOSE DACE

Rhinichthys cataractae

Other Names: none

Habitat: prefers stream riffles with rubble or gravel bottom; also found in lakes

Range: northern North America from Arctic Circle in Mackenzie River drainage south to northern Georgia, also in Rocky Mountains south into Rio Grande drainage of Texas and northern Mexico; in Colorado, native to the Arkansas and South Platte basins, introduced in the Colorado River system

Food: aquatic invertebrates, (immature aquatic insects picked from rocks), algae, fish eggs

Reproduction: matures in about 3 years; spawns over gravel bottom in shallow riffles when water temperature reaches about 53 degrees in late spring or early summer

Average Size: 3 to 5 inches

Records: none

Notes: A widespread little fish considered an important forage species for large predators, the Longnose Dace is well suited to darting among stones in swift-flowing streams. It feeds primarily on immature insects, which it picks off rocks. Adaptable, it survives in a variety of water conditions, from clear to turbid (cloudy).

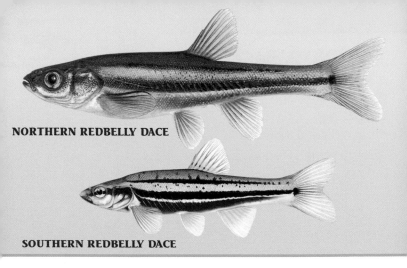

NORTHERN REDBELLY DACE

SOUTHERN REDBELLY DACE

Description: dark olive to brown back; two broad lateral bands on tan background; in breeding males, the tan turns orange and the belly becomes bright red or orange; blunt nose

Similar Species: Southern Redbelly Dace, Longnose Dace (pg. 54)

Northern Redbelly Dace	**Southern Redbelly Dace**	**Longnose Dace**
curved mouth, lower jaw slightly ahead of upper	straight mouth, upper jaw slightly ahead of lower jaw	upper jaw and snout extend well beyond lower jaw

NORTHERN REDBELLY DACE

Cyprinidae

Phoxinus eos

Other Names: redbelly, leatherback

Habitat: small slow-flowing streams and connected lakes; requires vegetation

Range: Northwest Territories to Hudson Bay, northeastern U.S. and eastern Canada; found in the South Platte basin in Colorado

Food: algae and other tiny bits of plant matter

Reproduction: from May to early August, a single female accompanied by several males will dart among masses of filamentous algae, laying 5 to 30 non-adhesive eggs at a time; males fertilize the eggs, which hatch in 8 to 10 days with no parental care

Average Size: 2 to 3 inches

Records: none

Notes: Dace are small fish that live in a variety of habitats. The Northern Redbelly Dace is a hardy fish that across its range survives in the acid water of bog-stained lakes and beaver ponds, as well as small streams. In Colorado it is rare, and a state endangered species. Breeding males are brightly colored and surpass many aquarium fish in beauty. Northern Redbelly Dace often hybridize with other species and sometimes form all-female populations. Its cousin, the Southern Redbelly Dace (*Phoxinus erythrogaster*), is also a state endangered species. It reportedly has disappeared from the wild but is present in captive populations.

Description: gray or olive-colored back; silver sides; white belly; slight bump behind head; caudal peduncle (area ahead of tail) is extremely thin

Similar Species: Humpback Chub (pg. 52)

Bonytail

Humpback Chub

slight bump behind head

pronounced hump behind head

BONYTAIL
Gila elegans

Cyprinidae

Other Names: none

Habitat: large, swift-flowing waters of the Colorado River system

Range: historically found in the Colorado River system, including the Yampa, Green, Gunnison and Colorado rivers, now limited to the Green River drainage in Utah and Mohave Reservoir in Arizona/Nevada; no known wild populations in Colorado remain

Food: insects, zooplankton, algae, plant debris

Reproduction: thought to spawn in late June and early July over gravel bottom

Size: 16 to 24 inches

Records: none

Notes: Considered the rarest of the rare Colorado River fish, the state and federally endangered Bonytail sports large fins and a streamlined body. It has been known to live nearly 50 years. Biologists believe widespread damming of the Colorado River reduced critical habitat. Competition from and predation by non-native fish species may also have contributed to the Bonytail's decline. The last reported wild fish from Colorado was caught in 1980. Restoration efforts include the reduction of non-native species, and restocking with hatchery fish.

Description: olive green to brown back; yellowish to dull silver sides brassy yellow in adults; white underside; often exhibits dusky stripe on side; complete lateral line

Similar Species: Fathead Minnow (pg. 66), Northern Redbelly Dace (pg. 56)

Brassy Minnow	Fathead Minnow	Brassy Minnow	Northern Redbelly Dace
first dorsal ray not split from other rays	first dorsal ray short, split from other rays	dusky lateral line	two dark lateral stripes

BRASSY MINNOW

Hybognathus hankinsoni

Cyprinidae

Other Names: none

Habitat: moderately clear tributary streams with sand or gravel bottoms; also found in small ponds; have been recorded in streams with slight current and silt bottoms

Range: north-central North America from the St. Lawrence River drainage across the Great Lakes and southern Canada south to Kansas, west to Colorado; in Colorado, native to Republican and South Platte basins; also reported in Colorado River drainage

Food: plankton, algae and organic matter from the bottom

Reproduction: matures at 2 to 3 years, at just over 2 inches in length; spawns in spring in and over weedgrowth; up to 15 males pursue a single female, fertilizing eggs

Average Size: 2 to 3½ inches

Records: none

Notes: Look for the Brassy Minnow in schools on or near bottom, often in association with Fathead Minnows and various shiners. Despite its ability to tolerate fluctuating temperature and oxygen conditions common in prairie streams, it is listed as threatened in Colorado.

NON-SPAWNING ADULT

SPAWNING MALE

Description: silver to light brown back and sides with scattered dark spots; white to silver belly; moderately stout body; bulbous snout overhanging mouth; fleshy lower lip partially covering hard shelf-like lower jaw; mature males have dark stripe along lower half of dorsal fin

Similar Species: Hornyhead Chub (pg. 50)

Central Stoneroller	Hornyhead Chub

mouth does not extend to eye	down-turned mouth extends to eye

CENTRAL STONEROLLER

Cyprinidae

Campostoma anomalum

Other Names: none

Habitat: pools and riffles, mainly in permanent streams but occasionally in plains streams with intermittent flows; prefers sand and gravel bottoms; requires current

Range: Colorado, Wyoming and northern Mexico north to Minnesota and south to Texas, east to the Appalachians; in Colorado, the Arkansas, Republican and South Platte basins

Food: plant debris and algae attached to stream bottoms

Reproduction: spawns when water temperature reaches 69 degrees; male constructs pit-type nest in shallow pool or riffle on fine gravel adjacent to deeper water; female deposits adhesive eggs in the pit, which the male fertilizes and covers

Average Size: 3 to 7 inches

Records: none

Notes: Another fascinating native Colorado species, the Central Stoneroller uses the odd, blade-like extension of its lower jaw to scrape algae and other plant matter from objects such as rocks and logs. It often forms large schools, which can be seen swirling in pools and runs as individual fish "graze" the bottom. Known to leap clear of the water for no apparent reason, then sink out of sight—particularly on warm days in spring or fall.

Description: grayish green to bronze back; silver to white sides and belly; fins may develop an orange coloration on breeding fish

Similar Species: Humpback Chub (pg. 52)

Colorado Pikeminnow

lacks hump behind head

Humpback Chub

pronounced hump behind head

COLORADO PIKEMINNOW

Cyprinidae

Ptychocheilus lucius

Other Names: Colorado squawfish

Habitat: large, fast-flowing, seasonally turbid (cloudy) rivers with warm backwaters

Range: Colorado River basin and most main tributaries; in Colorado, found in the Colorado, Dolores, Green, Gunnison, San Juan, White and Yampa rivers

Food: mostly fish, also insects, other invertebrates

Reproduction: migrates up to 200 miles to spawning areas such as riffles with gravel or rocky bottoms; spawns during spring and summer; eggs are broadcast randomly, there is no nest or parental care; eggs hatch in less than a week

Average Size: up to 48 inches and 60 pounds

Records: none

Notes: Largest member of the Minnow family native to North America, it historically reached lengths of 5 to 6 feet and weights of up to 80 pounds. Though a voracious predator, its only teeth are in a bony structure deep in the throat. Once common enough to support commercial fishing, it is listed as threatened in Colorado and endangered federally. Biologists blame dams and water diversion projects, which block access to spawning areas and lower water temperatures, along with the introduction of more than 40 species of non-native fish. Restoration efforts include restocking, dam bypasses, stabilizing stream flows to benefit juvenile fish and the removal of exotic species.

NON-SPAWNING ADULT

SPAWNING MALE

Description: olive back, golden yellow sides and white belly; dark lateral line widens to spot at base of tail; rounded snout and fins; no scales on head; dark blotch on dorsal fin

Similar Species: Hornyhead Chub (pg. 50), Creek Chub (pg. 46)

Fathead Minnow	Hornyhead Chub
upturned mouth	down-turned mouth

Fathead Minnow	Brassy Minnow
first dorsal ray short, split from other rays	first dorsal ray not split from other rays

Fathead Minnow	Creek Chub
anal fin has 7 rays	anal fin has 8 rays

FATHEAD MINNOW

Pimephales promelas

Cyprinidae

Other Names: blackhead, tuffy, mudminnow

Habitat: streams, ponds and lakes, particularly shallow, weedy or turbid (cloudy) areas lacking predators

Range: east of the Rocky Mountains in the U.S. and Canada; found throughout Colorado

Food: primarily algae and other plant matter, but will eat insects and copepods

Reproduction: from the time water temperatures reach 65 degrees in spring through September (unless they surpass 85 degrees), male prepares nest under rocks and sticks; female enters, turns upside down and lays adhesive eggs on the overhead object; after she leaves, the male fertilizes the eggs, which it then guards, fans with its fins and massages with a special, mucus-like pad on its back

Average Size: 3 to 4 inches

Records: none

Notes: The Fathead is one of Colorado's most numerous and widespread fish. Commonly used as bait, it withstands high temperatures and low oxygen levels. Prior to spawning, the male develops a dark coloration, breeding tubercles on its head that resemble small horns and a mucus-like patch on its back. During this phase, anglers report better luck when using female Fathead Minnows, perhaps due to their color or differing scent. Some biologists fear the Fathead could threaten native fish in areas where it has been introduced.

Description: back and upper sides dark greenish-gray; brassy sides; faint to dark lateral stripe; cream-colored belly; overall silvery appearance; pointed dorsal has 8 rays; complete lateral line; small mouth

Similar Species: Brassy Minnow (pg. 60)

Plains Minnow

Brassy Minnow

| pointed dorsal fin, first ray equal to or longer than second and third rays | rounded dorsal fin, first ray shorter than second and third rays |

PLAINS MINNOW

Hybognathus placitus

Other Names: none

Habitat: main channels of rivers; also found in pools below diversion projects

Range: plains states from Montana through Texas; in Colorado, the Arkansas and South Platte basins

Food: algae and other plant matter

Reproduction: matures at 1 year; spawns during high water in spring and summer, usually in turbid (cloudy) conditions; buoyant eggs tumble downstream with the current

Average Size: 3 to 5 inches

Records: none

Notes: A schooling fish that lives near the bottom, often congregating with various shiners and chubs, the Plains Minnow is not highly studied. It is thought to feed on algae and other organic matter from the bottom. It has a lengthy spawning season, with repeated spawning bouts triggered by rising water levels from rainfall. Currently on the state's endangered species list.

COMMON SHINER

GOLDEN SHINER

SAND SHINER

Description: silver body; dark green back, often with dark stripe; breeding males have bluish heads, rosy body and fins

Similar Species: Creek Chub (pg. 46), Golden Shiner, Sand Shiner

Common Shiner	Creek Chub	Sand Shiner
mouth barely extends to eye, which is large in relation to head	mouth extends to middle of eye, which is small in relation to head	mouth extends to eye, which is of moderate size

Common Shiner	Golden Shiner	Sand Shiner
usually 9 rays on anal fin	11 to 15 rays on anal fin	7 to 8 rays on anal fin

COMMON SHINER

Luxilus cornutus

Other Names: creek shiner

Habitat: lakes, rivers and streams; most common in the pools of streams and small rivers

Range: Midwest through eastern U.S. and Canada; in Colorado, the South Platte basin

Food: small insects, algae, zooplankton

Reproduction: beginning in late May, male prepares nest of small stones and gravel at the head of a stream riffle (may use the nest of a Creek Chub or Hornyhead Chub); other males are chased away, but females are courted with great flourish; it is generally thought that after spawning, both the male and female abandon the nest, but research has documented male Common Shiners and Hornyhead Chubs cooperating to defend a nest

Average Size: up to 6 inches

Records: none

Notes: The Common Shiner is a state threatened species. Elsewhere in its wide range, it is abundant to the point of being a popular baitfish. Research has shown that its diet varies through the year. It eats aquatic insects during the summer and winter, small fish in fall, and plant matter and fish in the spring. Depending on variations in color, it is similar in appearance to the closely related, native Sand Shiner (*Notropis stramineus*) and non-native Golden Shiner (*Notemigonus crysoleucas*).

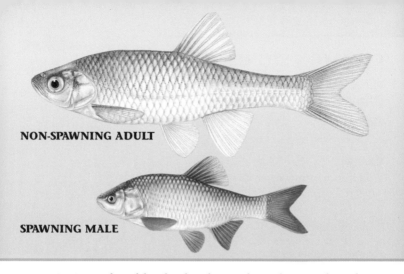

NON-SPAWNING ADULT

SPAWNING MALE

Description: silver blue back, silver sides; white underside; breeding males develop metallic blue coloration with bright orange-red on the head and fins (except dorsal)

Similar Species: Common Shiner (pg. 70), Golden Shiner

Red Shiner	Common Shiner	Red Shiner	Golden Shiner
front of dorsal fin midway between snout and tail base	front of dorsal fin closer to snout than base of tail	anal fin 8 to 10 rays, usually 9	anal fin 11 to 15 rays

RED SHINER

Cyprinella lutrensis

Other Names: none

Habitat: silty water with fluctuating flows

Range: middle to southwestern U.S. and Mexico, including Mississippi and western Gulf slope drainages; in Colorado, native to the Arkansas, Republican and South Platte basins, introduced in the west

Food: an opportunistic feeder, it eats a variety of algae and other plant matter, invertebrates and other small food items

Reproduction: spawns through spring and summer at water temperatures from 60 to 65 degrees; will spawn in a variety of areas: in vegetation and woody cover; over sand and gravel bottoms; even along the edges of the nests of other fish (such as Bluegills)

Average Size: up to 3 inches

Records: none

Notes: A schooling fish that spends much of its time in the middle of the water column or near the surface, the Red Shiner can tolerate pollution better than many species. It prefers backwater areas and deep pools where current speeds are less than one foot per second. Nationally, its range has expanded thanks to the bait and aquarium trade. Research has shown this highly adaptable fish will easily colonize new areas and hybridize with "local" shiners, threatening native fish populations.

Description: back and upper sides olive, brown or tan; dusky stripes on sides; fine black specks on head and body; dark vertical bar below eye; short, blunt snout and small mouth; incomplete lateral line; two dorsals; squared tail; spawning males develop bright orange coloration on lower sides, belly and gills; breeding females are dark tan

Similar Species: Iowa Darter (pg. 76), Johnny Darter (pg. 78), Orangethroat Darter (pg. 80)

Arkansas Darter	**Iowa Darter**	**Johnny Darter**	**Orangethroat Darter**
lateral line ends below spiny dorsal, with less than 20 pored scales	more than 55 lateral line scales	lateral line extends almost to base of tail	lateral line ends below soft dorsal, 42-50 lateral line scales

ARKANSAS DARTER

Etheostoma cragini

Other Names: none

Habitat: clear, shallow, spring-fed streams with moderate current, sandy bottom and an abundance of rooted aquatic vegetation

Range: native to the Arkansas River drainage, with localized populations in northwest Arkansas, eastern Colorado, southern Kansas, southwestern Missouri and north-central Oklahoma; in Colorado it is found in the Arkansas basin

Food: small aquatic invertebrates, plant matter including small seeds

Reproduction: matures at age 1 or less; spawns in spring and summer over course gravel bottom; eggs are deposited in open areas; no parental care

Average Size: 1½ to 2½ inches

Records: none

Notes: A cousin to the Sauger, Yellow Perch and Walleye, the Arkansas Darter is a rare, colorful little fish found in clear, spring-fed streams with plenty of weedy cover. Research has show adult darters prefer vegetation, while juveniles favor more open areas of the stream. Rare throughout its native range in the Arkansas River basin, it is listed as threatened in Colorado. Darters are affected by habitat loss due to pollution, overgrazing along streams and agricultural water use, both from the surface and underlying aquifer. They are also vulnerable to predators such as Northern Pike.

Description: greenish-brown back with faint blotches; sides have 9 to 12 vertical bars; dark spot under eye; bars become more pronounced and colors brighter on breeding males

Similar Species: Arkansas Darter (pg. 74), Johnny Darter (pg. 78), Orangethroat Darter (pg. 80)

Iowa Darter	**Arkansas Darter**	**Orangethroat Darter**
more than 55 lateral line scales	lateral line ends below spiny dorsal, less than 20 scales	lateral line ends below soft dorsal, 42-50 scales

Iowa Darter	**Johnny Darter**
blotches or bars on sides	X, Y and W markings

IOWA DARTER

Etheostoma exile

Other Names: weed darter, yellowbelly

Habitat: clear, slow-flowing streams and lakes that have undercut banks and some vegetation or an algae mat

Range: Saskatchewan to Quebec south to Colorado east to New York, Illinois and Ohio; in Colorado, it is found in some northeastern plains streams and some individual waters elsewhere, such as Eleven Mile Reservoir; introduced to Shadow Mountain Reservoir in the Colorado River basin

Food: insects, crustaceans

Reproduction: matures at 1 year; spawns May through July; adults deposit eggs on or among stones in shallow water; males establish breeding territories and females move from territory to territory, spawning with several males; eggs hatch in 12 to 26 days; no parental care

Average Size: $2^1/_2$ inches

Records: none

Notes: The Iowa Darter prefers slow-moving streams or still waters. In lakes it inhabits weedy shorelines. They are hard to see when still, but easy to spot when making a quick dart to a new resting place, where they perch on their pectoral fins. Iowa darters are very colorful, especially during the breeding season, and make fine aquarium fish, though they require live food. Males lose much of their color when held in captivity.

Description: tan to olive back and upper sides with dark blotches and speckling; sides tan to golden with X, Y and W patterns; breeding males darker with black bars

Similar Species: Arkansas Darter (pg. 74), Iowa Darter (pg. 76), Orangethroat Darter (pg. 80)

Johnny Darter	Arkansas Darter	Orangethroat Darter
lateral line extends almost to base of tail	lateral line ends below spiny dorsal, less than 20 scales	lateral line ends below soft dorsal, 42-50 scales

Johnny Darter	Iowa Darter
X, Y and W markings	blotches or bars on sides

JOHNNY DARTER

Etheostoma nigrum

Other Names: central Johnny darter

Habitat: rivers, streams and lakes

Range: Rocky Mountains east across Canada and the U.S. through the Great Lakes region; in Colorado, found in the North and South Platte drainages, and has been found in Haviland and Shadow Mountain reservoirs

Food: waterfleas, insect larvae, small crustaceans

Reproduction: spawns in April and May; male fans out nest beneath submerged object; females enter nest, turn upside down and deposit eggs on the underside of the nest; male guards eggs until hatching

Average Size: 2 to 3 inches

Records: none

Notes: Relatives of Yellow Perch and Walleye, darters are primarily stream fish that live among rocks in fast current. Small swim bladders allow them to sink rapidly to bottom after making a quick "dart," thus avoiding being swept away by the current. The Johnny Darter tolerates turbid (cloudy) conditions better than most darters, though it avoids very dirty streams and continuous strong flows. In Colorado it is found mainly in foothills areas but also occurs in some clear mountain lakes. In streams, it is often seen along banks or in shallow, flat runs, perching on its large pectoral fins, facing into the current.

Description: mottled green to yellowish brown back; dark bars (blue on male, brown on female); belly orange to white; dorsal fin and tail red with blue margin; large males develop blue anal fin, blue to black pelvic fin and two orange spots at base of tail; thin mark under eye; incomplete lateral line; breeding males develop blue and red bars, bright-orange throat

Similar Species: Arkansas Darter (pg. 74), Iowa Darter (pg. 76), Johnny Darter (pg. 78)

Orangethroat Darter	Arkansas Darter	Iowa Darter	Johnny Darter
lateral line ends below spiny dorsal, 42-50 lateral line scales	lateral line ends below spiny dorsal, with less than 20 pored scales	more than 55 lateral line scales	lateral line extends almost to base of tail

ORANGETHROAT DARTER

Etheostoma spectabile

Other Names: none

Habitat: most often occurs in small, clear, spring-fed streams with sand, gravel or rocky bottom and no silt, but will tolerate more turbid (cloudy), warmer water conditions

Range: widespread in U.S. central lowlands from southeast Iowa and southern Great Lakes and Kentucky south to Texas and west to Colorado; within the state, it is found in the Arikaree and Republican river drainages

Food: aquatic invertebrates, small crustaceans, fish eggs

Reproduction: matures at 2 years; spawns in spring and summer; female deposits eggs on gravel bottom in riffles; no further parental care; eggs hatch in 9 to 10 days

Average Size: 1 to 2½ inches

Records: none

Notes: The Orangethroat is a beautiful little fish, especially during the spawn, when the male sports bluish vertical bars, red blotches and multi-colored fins. Watch for its namesake orange throat and gill area. It is related to the Walleye and Yellow Perch but rarely surpasses much more than 2 inches in size. It has an average lifespan of 8 years. Like other darters it lacks a swim bladder, allowing it to "dart" quickly from one resting place to another without being swept away by the current. The Orangethroat is known as a colonizing species, one of the first fish to move into newly flooded streambeds.

SAUGER

SAUGEYE

Description: slender body; gray to dark silver or yellowish brown; dark blotches on sides, extending below the lateral line; may exhibit some white on lower margin of tail

Similar Species: Walleye (pg. 84)

Sauger	Saugeye	Walleye
spiny dorsal fin is spotted, lacks dark blotch on rear base	spiny dorsal fin has streaks, large dark spot on rear base	spiny dorsal fin lacks spots, has large dark spot on rear base
Sauger	**Saugeye**	**Walleye**
blotches on sides below lateral line	blotches on sides below lateral line	lacks blotches on sides below lateral line

SAUGER/SAUGEYE

Sander canadense, Sander vitreus x Sander canadense

Other Names: sand pike, spotfin pike, river pike, jackfish

Habitat: large lakes, rivers, often with turbid (cloudy) water

Range: Sauger—southern Canada, northern U.S. and larger reaches of the Mississippi, Missouri, Ohio and Tennessee river drainages; rare in Colorado; Saugeye—hybrid between Walleye and Sauger widely stocked in warmwater reservoirs

Food: small fish, aquatic insects, crayfish

Reproduction: Sauger—matures at 3 to 4 years; spawns as water temperature approaches 50 degrees; adults move into shallow waters of tributaries and headwaters to randomly deposit eggs over gravel; eggs hatch in about 12 to 18 days; Saugeye—occasionally reproduces with Walleye or Sauger

Average Size: 12 to 18 inches, 8 ounces to 2 pounds

Records: Sauger: state—3 pounds, 1 ounce; CF&I Reservoir No. 3, 1980; North American—8 pounds, 12 ounces; Lake Sakakawea, North Dakota, 1971; Saugeye: state—10 pounds, 14 ounces, John Martin Res., 2001; North American—15 pounds, 10 ounces, Fort Peck Reservoir, Montana, 1995

Notes: The Sauger is a slow grower, but despite its small stature it is an aggressive daytime feeder compared to the Walleye, and its fine-flavored flesh is top table fare. Hybridized with Walleye by fishery management biologists to produce the fast-growing, hard-fighting Saugeye, a popular sportfish which has been widely stocked in reservoirs across Colorado's eastern plains since the 1980s.

Description: silver or golden to dark olive brown in color; sharp canine teeth; dark spot at base of the three last spines in the dorsal fin; white spot on bottom lobe of tail

Similar Species: Sauger/Saugeye (pg. 82)

Walleye	**Saugeye**	**Sauger**
spiny dorsal fin lacks spots, has large dark spot on rear base	spiny dorsal fin has streaks, large dark spot on rear base	spiny dorsal fin is spotted, lacks dark blotch on rear base
Walleye	**Saugeye**	**Sauger**
lacks blotches on sides below lateral line	blotches on sides below lateral line	blotches on sides below lateral line

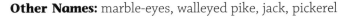
WALLEYE

Sander vitreus

Other Names: marble-eyes, walleyed pike, jack, pickerel

Habitat: large lakes, reservoirs and rivers

Range: originally northern U.S. and Canada, now widely stocked; introduced in warmwater Colorado reservoirs

Food: mainly small fish such as juvenile Yellow Perch, White Suckers, Rainbow Smelt and various minnows, depending on forage base and opportunity; also eats insects, crayfish, leeches and other small prey

Reproduction: matures at 2 to 4 years; spawns at night in tributary streams or wind- or current-washed lake shoals when spring water temperatures reach 40 to 50 degrees; prefers rubble bottom in shallow water; groups of adults broadcast eggs, which typically hatch in 12 to 18 days

Average Size: 14 to 17 inches, 1 to 3 pounds

Records: state—18 pounds, 3 ounces, Standley Lake, 1997; North American—22 pounds, 11 ounces, Greer's Ferry Lake, Arkansas, 1982

Notes: Though not native, the Walleye has become one of Colorado's top sportfish since its introduction in 1949. It puts up a decent fight, particularly on light tackle, and its white fillets rank high in table quality. Fishing opportunities are widespread in warmwater reservoirs. Boulder, Chatfield and Pueblo are good options, and there is a noted trophy Walleye fishery at Cherry Creek Reservoir, with peak fishing in mid-May to June near the dam and island.

Description: 6 to 9 dark, vertical bars on bright yellowish green to orange background; long dorsal with two distinct lobes; lower fins have a yellow to orange tinge

Similar Species: Walleye (pg. 84)

Yellow Perch	Walleye
lacks large white spot on tail	prominent white spot on tail

Percidae

YELLOW PERCH

Perca flavescens

Other Names: ringed, striped or jack perch, green hornet

Habitat: warm to cool lakes and slow-flowing streams, adults prefer clear open water

Range: widely introduced in northern U.S. and southern Canada; common in warmwater lakes across Colorado

Food: small fish, insects, snails, leeches and crayfish

Reproduction: matures at 2 years; spawns at night in shallow, weedy areas in spring when water warms to 45 to 50 degrees; female drapes gelatinous ribbons of eggs over submerged vegetation; eggs incubate 10 to 20 days

Average Size: 8 to 11 inches, 6 to 10 ounces

Records: state—2 pounds, 5 ounces, Gravel Pit, Larimer County, 1983 North American—4 pounds, 3 ounces, Bordentown, New Jersey, 1865

Notes: A non-native, the Yellow Perch is common in Colorado and may be our most abundant game fish. Small ones are considered a nuisance but those about 10 inches or more in length are popular with anglers. Excellent table quality. Perch travel in schools of about the same age class and size. They are an important link in the food web, serving as important forage for Walleyes, Northern Pike, Largemouth Bass and other predators. In turn, overfishing top predators can lead to a population of "stunted" or undersized perch. In some cases, illegally stocked Yellow Perch have had a detrimental effect on trout and salmon populations.

Description: long body with dorsal fin near tail; head is long and flattened in front, forming a duck-like snout; dark green back, light green sides with bean-shaped light spots; Silver Pike are a rare, silver colored race of Northern Pike

Similar Species: Tiger Muskie (pg. 90)

Northern Pike   **Tiger Muskie**

light spots on   dark marks on
dark back-   light background   ground

NORTHERN PIKE

Esocidae

Esox lucius

Other Names: pickerel, jack, 'gator, hammerhandle, snot rocket

Habitat: lakes, streams and rivers (though it avoids strong currents); often found near weeds but will range widely in open water; small pike tolerate water temperatures up to 70 degrees but larger fish prefer 55 degrees or less

Range: northern Europe, Asia and North America; in Colorado, introduced in large lakes and rivers statewide

Food: small fish, frogs, crayfish and other small creatures; typically feeds on live prey but will scavenge dead fish

Reproduction: matures at 2 years; spawns in tributaries and marshes at 34- to 40-degree water temperatures; attended by 1 to 3 males, female deposits eggs in shallow vegetation; eggs hatch in about 14 days

Average Size: 18 to 24 inches, 2 to 5 pounds

Records: state—30 pounds, 11 ounces, Stagecoach Reservoir, 2006; North American—46 pounds, 2 ounces, Sacandaga Reservoir, New York, 1940

Notes: A voracious predator, the Northern Pike is a daytime sight feeder that often lies in wait in weedy cover, capturing prey with a fast lunge. Lakes with ample forage, areas of oxygen-rich cool water in summer and low harvest tend to offer the best chance at trophy pike. Eagerly hits natural and artificial baits and fights hard when hooked. Pike can deplete native fish and stocked trout populations; such has been the case in some of Colorado's coldwater lakes.

89

Description: torpedo-shaped body; dorsal fin near tail; sides typically silver to silver-green with tiger-like bars on light background; rounded lobes on fins and tail

Similar Species: Northern Pike (pg. 88)

Tiger Muskie   **Northern Pike**

tiger bars   light marks
on light   on dark
background   background

TIGER MUSKIE

Esox masquinongy x *Esox lucius*

Other Names: lunge

Habitat: large, clear lakes with extensive weedbeds; also medium to large rivers with slow currents and deep pools

Range: a hybrid species, no native range; stocked in a variety of Colorado waters

Food: mainly fish

Reproduction: usually sterile, non-reproducing

Average Size: 30 to 42 inches, 10 to 20 pounds

Records: state—40 pounds, 2 ounces, Quincy Reservoir, 1994; North American—51 pounds, 3 ounces, Lac Vieux Desert, Michigan/Wisconsin, 1919

Notes: The hybrid offspring of a Northern Pike and Muskellunge, the Tiger Muskie is a voracious predator and popular game fish. Introduced in Colorado in the 1980s to control suckers and carp, as well as provide trophy-caliber fishing opportunities, it can top 40 pounds. The Tiger Muskie takes on some qualities of both its carnivorous parents, and can be found around weedbeds and in open water, stalking prey and shadowing schools of baitfish.

Description: dark brown to olive back; sides lighter, fading to cream belly; sides have light red or pink spots on a dark background; cream border on pelvic and anal fins; breeding colors range from intense gold to red-orange

Similar Species: Brook Trout (pg. 94); Kokanee Salmon (pg. 108)

Arctic Char	**Brook Trout**	**Arctic Char**	**Kokanee Salmon**
back lacks wormlike markings	wormlike markings on back	anal fin not longer than deep	anal fin longer than it is deep

ARCTIC CHAR

Salvelinus alpinus

Other Names: blueback char, blueback trout

Habitat: deep pools and runs of coldwater rivers; deep, cold, clear areas of lakes with ample oxygen and temperatures between the mid-40s and 50 degrees

Range: coastal waters in Pacific, Arctic and Atlantic drainages from Alaska to Newfoundland, south to New England; in Colorado, stocked in Dillon Reservoir

Food: crustaceans, insects, plankton, small fish

Reproduction: typically matures in 2 to 4 years; spawns over rock or gravel shoals August through October, when water temperatures drop below 50; in some lake-run populations, adults gather near inlet streams before moving back into the lake to spawn; thought to spawn in alternate years; does not build nest or "redd"

Average Size: 13 to 20 inches, 1 to 4 pound

Records: state—3 pounds, 12 ounces, Dillon Reservoir, 1994; North American—32 pounds, 9 ounces, Tree River, N.W.T., Canada, 1981

Notes: The Arctic Char is native to the polar regions of North America into the New England states in the Northeast. It occurs in anadromous sea-run populations and landlocked forms. It was stocked in Colorado's Dillon Reservoir as part of efforts to establish a coldwater sportfishery. Though the last stocking was in 1998, it is still possible to encounter an Arctic Char in the lake.

Description: back is olive, blue-gray to black with wormlike markings; sides bronze to olive with red spots tinged light brown; lower fins red-orange with white leading edge; tail squared or slightly forked

Similar Species: Brown Trout (pg. 96), Rainbow Trout (pg. 104), Lake Trout (pg. 102), Splake (pg. 102)

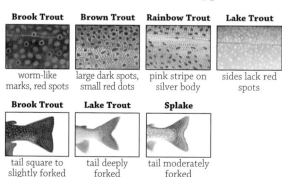

Brook Trout	**Brown Trout**	**Rainbow Trout**	**Lake Trout**
worm-like marks, red spots	large dark spots, small red dots	pink stripe on silver body	sides lack red spots

Brook Trout	**Lake Trout**	**Splake**
tail square to slightly forked	tail deeply forked	tail moderately forked

BROOK TROUT

Salvelinus fontinalis

Other Names: speckled, squaretail or coaster trout, brookie

Habitat: cool, clear high elevation streams and small lakes with sand or gravel bottoms and moderate vegetation; prefers water temperatures of 50 to 60 degrees

Range: Great Lakes region north to Labrador, south through the Appalachians to Georgia; introduced into the western U.S., Canada, Europe and South America; found across Colorado in suitable habitat

Food: insects, small fish, leeches, crustaceans

Reproduction: spawns in late fall at 40- to 49-degree water temperatures on gravel bars in stream riffles and in lakes where springs aerate eggs; female builds 4- to 12-inch-deep nest (male may guard during construction) in gravel, then buries fertilized eggs, which hatch in 50 to 150 days

Average Size: 8 to 10 inches, 8 ounces

Records: state—7 pounds, 10 ounces, Upper Cataract Lake, 1947; North American—14 pounds, 8 ounces, Nipigon River, Ontario, 1916

Notes: Introduced to Colorado in the late 1800s, this striking little trout—with its voracious appetite, strong runs and delicate flavor—is prized by trout fishermen. It is very prolific; biologists have documented up to 3,500 fish per acre in some streams. Can cause declines in native trout populations through direct competition for resources.

BROWN TROUT

TIGER TROUT

Description: golden-brown to olive back and sides; large dark spots on sides, dorsal fin and sometimes upper lobe of tail; red spots with light halos scattered along sides

Similar Species: Rainbow Trout (pg. 104), Lake Trout (pg. 102), Brook Trout (pg. 94), Tiger Trout

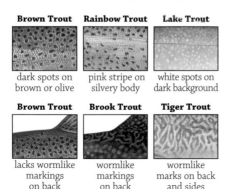

Brown Trout	Rainbow Trout	Lake Trout
dark spots on brown or olive	pink stripe on silvery body	white spots on dark background

Brown Trout	Brook Trout	Tiger Trout
lacks wormlike markings on back	wormlike markings on back	wormlike marks on back and sides

BROWN TROUT

Salmo trutta

Other Names: German brown, Loch Leven or spotted trout

Habitat: open ocean near spawning streams and clear, cold, gravel-bottomed streams; shallow areas of large reservoirs

Range: native to Europe from the Mediterranean to Arctic Norway and Siberia, widely introduced worldwide; found in streams and impoundments throughout Colorado

Food: insects, crayfish, small fish

Reproduction: spawns October through December in stream headwaters and tributaries; stream mouths are used when migration is blocked; female fans out saucer-shaped nest, which male guards until spawning; female covers eggs

Average Size: 11 to 20 inches, 2 to 6 pounds

Records: state—30 pounds, 8 ounces, Roaring Judy Ponds, 1988; North American—40 pounds, 4 ounces, Little Red River River, Arkansas, 1992

Notes: This European trout was brought to Colorado in the 1890s. It is a secretive, hard-to-catch fish that fights hard and has a fine, delicate flavor. Often feeds aggressively on cloudy, rainy days and at night. Though it can survive in 80-degree water for a short time, it prefers the 50s to lower 60s. May hybridize with Brook Trout to produce sterile Tiger Trout. Colorado has many top-notch Brown Trout fisheries. The South Platte River from Cheesman Reservoir to Strontia Springs Reservoir, and the Arkansas River from Buena Vista to Salida, are among the best in North America.

97

Description: brown to olive back; golden yellowish sides with crimson stripe and dark markings along lateral line; red gill covers; adipose fin; triangular dorsal fin

Similar Species: Brook Trout (pg. 94), Greenback Cutthroat Trout (pg. 100)

Golden Trout	Brook Trout	Golden Trout	Greenback Cutthroat
red band with dark marks on side	lacks defined red band and dark marks	white tip on anal, dorsal and pelvic fins	lacks white tip on anal, dorsal and pelvic fins

GOLDEN TROUT

Oncorhynchus aguabonita

Other Names: mountain trout

Habitat: clean, clear lakes and streams

Range: native to California; introduced in some high-elevation Colorado lakes

Food: insects, crustaceans

Reproduction: spawns in summer at water temperatures of about 50 degrees; female fans out spawning bed or "redd" in tributary stream; no parental care

Average Size: 16 to 20 inches

Records: state—3 pounds, 12 ounces, Kelly Lake, 1979; North American—11 pounds, 4 ounces, Cook Lake, Wyoming, 1948

Notes: A California native, the Golden Trout has been stocked in some Colorado lakes in the high country. It is a close relative of the Rainbow Trout. Considered one of the most beautiful of game fish, its striking gold and crimson coloration is hard to mistake. Look for "parr marks"—dark oval-shaped markings on the side along the lateral line, particularly in stream-run fish. Though oily, the fillets are excellent fresh or smoked.

GREENBACK CUTTHROAT

COLORADO RIVER CUTTHROAT

RIO GRANDE CUTTHROAT

SNAKE RIVER CUTTHROAT

Description: blood-red stripes on each side of throat under jaw; round, dark spots on sides and tail; breeding males develop crimson head, side and belly

Similar Species: Brook Trout (pg. 94), Brown Trout (pg. 96), Golden Trout (pg. 98), Rainbow Trout (pg. 104)

All Cutthroats	**Brook Trout***	**Greenback Cutthroat**	**Golden Trout**
red slash mark on throat	lacks red slash mark on throat	lacks white tip on anal, dorsal and pelvic fins	white tip on anal, dorsal and pelvic fins

Native Cutthroats	**Snake River Cutthroat**
large, dark spots	small, fine spots

Also valid for Brown and Rainbow Trout.

GREENBACK CUTTHROAT TROUT *Oncorhynchus clarki stomias*

Other Names: 'cutt, mountain trout

Habitat: clear, cold (mid-50s to low 60s), swift, gravel-bottom headwater streams with overhanging banks or vegetation; also mountain lakes with abundant insect life

Range: native to Arkansas and South Platte river systems in Colorado and part of Wyoming

Food: freshwater shrimp, aquatic and terrestrial insects, fish

Reproduction: spawns from late May to mid-July, depending on elevation; female excavates 3- to 8-inch-deep depression in gravel; a single female may lay up to 6,000 eggs

Average Size: 12 inches, 1 to 2 pounds

Records: state—(native) 16 pounds, Twin Lakes, 1964; (Snake River strain) 17 pounds, 2.6 ounces, Blue River, 2005; North American—(*Oncorhynchus clarki*) 41 pounds, Pyramid Lake, Nevada, 1925

Notes: One of numerous Cutthroat subspecies. Thought extinct in 1937. Remnant populations were later discovered and it was named the state fish in 1994. Now listed as threatened. Other subspecies in the state include the native Colorado River and Rio Grande strains, and non-native Snake River Cutthroat. Field identification of native fish is largely a matter of location. For the most part, Greenbacks are found in the Arkansas and South Platte drainages, while the Colorado River strain is west of the continental divide—except for the Rio Grande basin, which holds its namesake subspecies.

101

LAKE TROUT

SPLAKE

Description: dark gray to gray-green on head, back, top fins and tail; white spots on sides and unpaired fins; deeply forked tail; inside of mouth is white

Similar Species: Brook Trout (pg. 94), Splake

Lake Trout

sides lack wormlike markings

Brook Trout

wormlike marks on back

Lake Trout

tail deeply forked

Brook Trout

tail square to slightly forked

Splake

tail moderately forked

LAKE TROUT
Salvelinus namaycush

Other Names: mackinaw, togue, laker, great gray trout

Habitat: oxygen-rich cold water (prefers 48 to 52 degrees); deep, clear, infertile lakes with rocky bottoms

Range: northeastern U.S. and Great Lakes north through Canada to Alaska; introduced in Rocky Mountains; stocked in coldwater fisheries in Colorado

Food: small fish, insects, crustaceans

Reproduction: females scatter eggs over rocky lake bottoms, on shoals or reefs, when autumn water temperature falls below 50 degrees; eggs incubate over winter and hatch in March or April when water reaches mid to upper 30s

Average Size: 16 to 24 inches, 7 to 10 pounds

Records: state—46 pounds, 14.6 ounces, Blue Mesa Reservoir, 2003; North American—72 pounds, 4 ounces; Great Bear Lake, N.W.T., Canada, 1995

Notes: This hard-fighting member of the Char family is the largest trout in North America. It is long-lived and slow-growing in much of its native range. However, research has shown fast growth in at least one Colorado fishery. Biologists using tiny ear bones—or otoliths—to determine the age of Lake Trout in Blue Mesa Reservoir found they grow quickly, reaching up to 32 inches in length in 10 years and 40 inches in 20 years. Biologists credit Blue Mesa's ample supply of protein- and calorie-rich Rainbow Trout and Kokanee Salmon. Can hybridize with Brook Trout to produce Splake.

Description: blue-green to brown head and back; silver lower sides, often with pink to rose stripe; sides, back, dorsal fins and tail are covered with small black spots

Similar Species: Brook Trout (pg. 94), Brown Trout (pg. 96)

Rainbow Trout	Brook Trout	Rainbow Trout	Brown Trout

| lacks wormlike markings | wormlike marks on back | pinkish stripe on silvery body | sides lack pinkish stripe |

RAINBOW TROUT

Oncorhynchus mykiss

Other Names: steelhead, Pacific trout, silver trout

Habitat: prefers whitewater in cool streams and coastal regions of large lakes, tolerates smaller cool, clear lakes

Range: Pacific Ocean and coastal streams from Mexico to Alaska and northeast Russia, introduced worldwide; stocked in cooler streams and lakes across Colorado

Food: insects, small crustaceans, fish

Reproduction: predominantly spring spawners but some fall spawning varieties exist; female builds nest in well-aerated gravel in streams and lakes

Average Size: 20 inches, 3 to 8 pounds

Records: state—19 pounds, 10 ounces, Morrow Point Reservoir, 2003; North American—(inland) 37 pounds, Lake Pend Oreille, Idaho, 1947

Notes: This Pacific trout was first stocked in Colorado in the 1880s. Known for acrobatic battles and excellent table quality. Reproduces in some streams and lakes but much of the state's fishery is maintained by stocking; each year, the DOW stocks approximately 4.5 million rainbows over 8 inches in length. Spinney Mountain Reservoir is a great choice for consistent 'bows topping 16 inches. The South Platte, Rio Grande (from Rio Grande Reservoir to Del Norte) and Arkansas rivers also hold world-class Rainbow Trout fishing; the "blizzard" caddis fly hatch on the Arkansas in late April to early May is particularly famous.

Description: striking iridescent appearance; sail-like dorsal fin is dusky brown to dark gray with rows of red, purple or bluish spots; dark back; grayish silver sides with dark spots; pelvic fins marked with pink to orange stripes

Similar Species: Mountain Whitefish (pg. 112)

Arctic Grayling

spotted, sail-like dorsal fin

Mountain Whitefish

small triangular dorsal fin lacks spots

ARCTIC GRAYLING
Thymallus arcticus

Other Names: bluefish, grayling, sailfin

Habitat: clear, cold lakes and rivers; prefers water temperatures at or below 50 degrees

Range: northern Canada and Alaska, with subspecies in Michigan (now extinct) and Montana; introduced into coldwater lakes and high backcountry fisheries in Colorado

Food: drifting aquatic insects such as mayflies and caddis flies; also terrestrial insects, fish eggs, crustaceans, fish

Reproduction: spawns over gravel or rock in tributary streams when spring water temperatures reach 44 to 50 degrees

Average Size: 12 to 16 inches, 8 to 16 ounces

Records: state—1 pound, 10 ounces, Lower Big Creek Lake, 2002; North American—5 pounds, 15 ounces, Katseyedie River, Northwest Territories, 1967

Notes: Arctic Grayling have been stocked in Colorado since the 1890s and are available to anglers in select fisheries, such as Joe Wright Reservoir west of Fort Collins. While its beautiful, shimmering coloration is remarkable, the sail-like dorsal fin is its trademark. The male's dorsal is longer than the female's, for good reason. He wraps it around her during spawning, ensuring as many eggs as possible are fertilized. This is an important trait because grayling don't produce as much eggs and milt as other fish. Has excellent distance vision for spotting prey, but poor eyesight at close range and may make several passes at a lure before connecting.

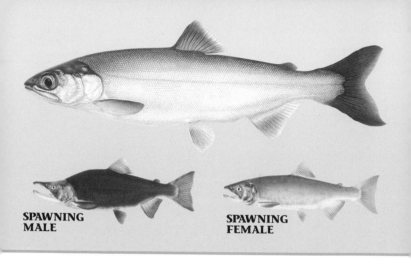

SPAWNING MALE

SPAWNING FEMALE

Description: bluish green back, often with small black dots; sides bright silver; anal fin has 13 to 17 rays and the base is longer than the base of the dorsal fin; during the spawning season, both sexes develop reddish sides and green heads; the male's coloration is brighter and the female may appear almost silver-purple; breeding male also develops a humped back and hooked jaw or kype

Similar Species: Mountain Whitefish (pg. 112), Rainbow Trout (pg. 104)

Kokanee Salmon

Mountain Whitefish

jaw extends beyond center of eye

jaw does not extend beyond center of eye

Kokanee Salmon

Rainbow Trout

tail lacks spots

many spots on both lobes of tail

KOKANEE SALMON

Oncorhynchus nerka

Other Names: koke, red salmon, silver trout, sockeye

Habitat: large, clear, cold lakes and reservoirs; prefers water temperatures in the low to mid 50s

Range: native to the Arctic and Pacific drainages from Alaska to Sacramento River drainage, California; widely introduced in the U.S.; in Colorado, introduced in coldwater reservoirs

Food: zooplankton, small crustaceans, aquatic insects

Reproduction: pairs spawn in fall, usually in tributary streams; female digs bed or "redd" in gravel, sand or rubble; parents guard nest until death, soon after spawning

Average Size: 1 to 3 pounds

Records: state—6 pounds, 13 ounces, Spinney Mountain Reservoir, 1986; North American—9 pounds, 6 ounces, Okanagan Lake, British Columbia, 1988

Notes: A smaller, landlocked version of the Pacific Sockeye Salmon, the Kokanee was introduced to Colorado in 1951 with eggs from Flathead Lake, Montana. Colorado began self-sufficient egg production in 1958, mainly from Lake Granby and Blue Mesa. The only Pacific salmon to mature in freshwater. Anglers often fish Kokanee in summer by trolling cowbell rigs at mid-range depths, looking for tight pods that school by water temperature; ice fishing is another fun option, and snagging seasons are offered in some streams. Table quality is excellent. Elevenmile Reservoir produces some of Colorado's largest Kokanee.

Description: silver with dark brown to olive back and tail; snout protrudes past lower jaw; mouth is small, with two small flaps between the openings of each nostril

Similar Species: Mountain Whitefish (pg. 112)

Lake Whitefish

tip of snout above lower edge of eye

Mountain Whitefish

tip of snout below eye

LAKE WHITEFISH

Salmonidae

Coregonus clupeaformis

Other Names: eastern, common or Great Lakes whitefish, gizzard fish, Sault whitefish

Habitat: large, deep, clean lakes with cool, oxygen-rich depths during the summer

Range: from the Great Lakes north across North America; rare in Colorado

Food: zooplankton, insects, small fish

Reproduction: spawns on shallow gravel bars in late fall when water temperatures reach the low 30s; occasionally ascends streams to spawn

Average Size: 18 inches, 3 to 5 pounds

Records: state—none; North American—15 pounds, 6 ounces, Clear Lake, Ontario, 1983

Notes: The largest whitefish in North America. Just before the ice forms in the fall, Lake Whitefish enter shallows to spawn and were often speared or netted at this time. Considered one of the finest food fish from freshwater. Also an important forage species.

Description: dark bluish silver to brown back; silver sides; white belly; small head for body size; mouth is under snout; adipose fin; larger scales than trout

Similar Species: Arctic Grayling (pg. 106), Kokanee Salmon (pg. 108), Lake Whitefish (pg. 110)

Mountain Whitefish	Kokanee Salmon	Mountain Whitefish	Arctic Grayling
jaw does not extend beyond center of eye	jaw extends beyond center of eye	small triangular dorsal fin lacks spots	spotted, sail-like dorsal fin

Mountain Whitefish	Lake Whitefish
tip of snout below eye	snout tip above lower edge of eye

MOUNTAIN WHITEFISH

Prosopium williamsoni

Other Names: Rocky Mountain whitefish

Habitat: pools and slow-flowing stretches of mid-size to large mountain streams; also found in clear, cold lakes and reservoirs; prefers water temperatures below 52 degrees

Range: native to western U.S. and Canada; in Colorado native to the White and Yampa rivers, introduced into Cache la Poudre and Roaring Fork drainages; found in many lakes

Food: mainly a bottom-feeder on insects and crustaceans at dusk and night, but will feed at the surface during the day

Reproduction: matures at 3 years; spawns in streams and along lake shorelines in fall at water temperatures at or below 44 degrees; scatters eggs over gravel or rubble; no nest is built; eggs hatch the following March

Average Size: 10 to 18 inches, 1 to 2 pounds

Records: state—5 pounds, 2 ounces, Roaring Fork River, 1982; North American—5 pounds, 14 ounces, Island Park Reservoir, Idaho, 1997

Notes: The Mountain Whitefish's downturned mouth is perfect for vacuuming up bottom-dwelling insects and other food. Though it feeds mostly on bottom, it will rise to feed on the surface during the day and is a willing striker on flies and natural baits. Be forewarned, though, its small, delicate mouth makes hooking and landing this spirited fighter a challenge. Its meat is oily but good when eaten fresh and absolutely delicious smoked.

MOTTLED SCULPIN

ROUND GOBY

Description: blotchy brown coloration; large mouth; eyes set almost on top of the broad head; large, winglike pectoral fins; lacks scales

Similar Species: Round Goby (non-native)

Mottled Sculpin	Round Goby
lacks scales; pelvic fins not fused together	scales on body; pelvic fins fused

MOTTLED SCULPIN

Cottus bairdii

Other Names: common sculpin, muddler, gudgeon

Habitat: cool, hard-water streams and clear lakes; favors areas with rocks or vegetation

Range: eastern U.S. through Canada to Hudson Bay and the Rockies; in Colorado, the western slope of Animas, Colorado, Dolores, San Juan, White and Yampa drainages

Food: aquatic invertebrates, fish eggs, small fish

Reproduction: spawns in spring at water temperatures of 63 to 74 degrees; male fans out cavity beneath a rock, ledge or log and attracts females through courtship displays such as head nodding, head shaking and gill cover raising; spawning fish turn upside down and deposit eggs on underside of nest cover; male guards and cleans the nest after spawning

Average Size: 4 to 5 inches

Records: none

Notes: Though it favors clear, cool, fast-flowing mountain streams (averaging 68 degrees), the Mottled Sculpin is also found in areas of the Gunnison and other rivers where summer water temperatures surpass 80 degrees. It is an important food source for a variety of predators, which it avoids by modifying its body color to blend in with the surroundings. Look for sculpins under rocks in streams. Very similar to exotic Round Goby, *Apollonia (Neogobius) melanostomus*, a native of Eurasia reported in nine states and Canada but as yet undocumented in Colorado.

Description: long, thin body; sides silvery with bright silver stripe; beak-like, upturned mouth; two dorsal fins

Similar Species: Common Shiner (pg. 70), Rainbow Smelt (pg. 118)

Brook Silverside	Common Shiner	Rainbow Smelt
two dorsal fins	single dorsal fin	single dorsal fin

BROOK SILVERSIDE

Labidesthes sicculus

Other Names: needlenose or stick minnow, skipjack, friar

Habitat: surface areas of clear to slightly turbid (cloudy), warm lakes and slack-current or slow-flowing portions of large streams and rivers; uncommon in thick weedgrowth

Range: southeastern U.S. to the Great Lakes; in Colorado, it has been reported in the South Platte drainage

Food: aquatic and flying insects, spiders

Reproduction: spawns in late spring and early summer; males school near the surface and pair with females; as the pair swims or glides downward, eggs are laid in sticky strings that attach to vegetation or the bottom; most adults die soon after spawning

Average Size: 3 to 4 inches

Records: none

Notes: The Brook Silverside spends much of its short life (its maximum lifespan is about 17 months) cruising within a few inches of the surface, and is thought never to venture more than a few feet deep. Its flat head and upturned mouth are adaptations to topwater feeding. Most active during the day, it is often observed darting about in small schools; individual fish often leap from the water in pursuit of prey. A creature of the light, the Brook Silverside lies motionless near the surface on dark nights. Its activity level picks up considerably on moonlit evenings, and it is attracted to artificial lights shining on the water.

117

Description: large mouth with prominent teeth; jaw extends to rear margin of the eye; dark green back; violet-blue sides and white belly; deeply forked tail; adipose fin

Similar Species: Mountain Whitefish (pg. 112), Common Shiner (pg. 70), Brook Silverside (pg. 116)

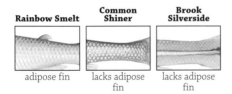

Rainbow Smelt

adipose fin

Common Shiner

lacks adipose fin

Brook Silverside

lacks adipose fin

RAINBOW SMELT

Osmerus mordax

Other Names: ice or frost fish, lake herring, leefish

Habitat: open oceans and large lakes, tributaries at spawning

Range: coastal Pacific, Atlantic and Arctic Oceans, landlocked in northeast U.S. and southeast Canada; in Colorado, introduced in the Arkansas and South Platte drainages and headwaters of the Colorado basin

Food: crustaceans, insect larvae, small fish

Reproduction: spawning takes place in May, at night, in the first mile of tributary streams

Average Size: 8 to 10 inches

Records: none

Notes: A saltwater fish that enters freshwater to spawn, the Rainbow Smelt has been widely introduced in New York, the upper Midwest, Montana, Idaho and Colorado. Where it has been introduced in inland lakes, the Rainbow Smelt is excellent forage for large predators such as Walleyes, but some biologists link it to eventual declines in predator populations, due to predation on young game fish or competition for food. In Horsetooth Reservoir, Walleye populations did well shortly after its arrival in 1983, but by 1988, Walleye recruitment ceased. The introduction of hybrid Striped Bass (Wipers) and a resurgence in Walleye numbers has since helped rein in the Rainbow Smelt.

119

BROOK STICKLEBACK

NINESPINE STICKLEBACK

Description: brown with torpedo-shaped body and narrow caudal peduncle (area just before the tail); front portion of dorsal fin has short, separated spines; pelvic fins are abdominal and reduced to a single spine; small, sharp teeth

Similar Species: Ninespine Stickleback

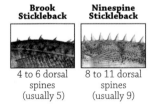

Brook Stickleback	Ninespine Stickleback
4 to 6 dorsal spines (usually 5)	8 to 11 dorsal spines (usually 9)

BROOK STICKLEBACK

Gasterosteidae

Culaea inconstans

Other Names: common stickleback, spiny minnow

Habitat: clear, cool streams with slow flows; ponds with an abundance of filamentous algae and other vegetation

Range: Kansas through the northern U.S. and Canada; in Colorado, the Arkansas and South Platte basins

Food: insects, fish eggs, juvenile fish, occasionally algae

Reproduction: in spring and summer, at water temperatures above 66 degrees, male builds a golf-ball-sized, globular nest of sticks, algae and other plant matter on submerged vegetation; females deposit eggs and depart, often plowing a hole in the side of the nest in the process; the male repairs any damage and viciously guards the eggs until hatching; an ambitious male may build a second, larger nest and transfer the eggs there by mouth

Average Size: 1½ to 2½ inches

Records: none

Notes: An interesting little carnivore, the Brook Stickleback sometimes ends up in anglers' bait pails mixed in with small Fatheads or "crappie minnows." Though it is often discarded in disgust, it works well as bait. The pugnacious predators also make fun aquarium fish (where legal). Native to Colorado, it is relatively common and holds no special conservation status. Related to the Ninespine Stickleback (*Pungitius pungitius*), a non-native fish reportedly found in bait buckets in the South Platte drainage.

Description: brown, slate to olive back; silvery sides; white underside; bump in middle of lower lip; long, sickle-like dorsal fin; dusky dorsal fin and tail; lower fins white to pinkish yellow

Similar Species: Common Carp (pg. 42)

River Carpsucker

Common Carp

mouth lacks barbels

barbels below mouth

RIVER CARPSUCKER

Carpiodes carpio

Other Names: white or silver carp, quillback

Habitat: quiet, soft-bottomed pools, backwaters and oxbows of large, slow-flowing streams; seldom seen in main channel areas; also found in eastern Colorado reservoirs; prefers turbid (cloudy) conditions

Range: Mississippi River basin from Pennsylvania to Montana, south to Louisiana; Gulf Slope drainage from Louisiana to Texas and New Mexico; also found in Mexico; in Colorado, the Arkansas and South Platte basins

Food: algae and other plant matter, crustaceans, insects

Reproduction: matures at 2 to 3 years; spawns in late spring and summer along lake and stream shorelines; scattered randomly, eggs hatch in 8 to 15 days; no parental care

Average Size: 18 to 19 inches, 2 to 3 pounds

Records: North American—12 pounds, 10 ounces, Boysen Reservoir, Wyoming, 2005

Notes: Large schools of adult River Carpsuckers will roam throughout a reservoir, consuming massive amounts of algae. Young fish tend to favor backwater areas of rivers or streams. While juveniles may be of some importance as food for larger predators, they quickly grow to sizes too big for most other fish to eat. Large specimens occasionally reach 10 pounds. Rarely caught on hook and line.

Description: dark back; grayish-blue to tan or yellowish sides; head of adults often develops bluish color; long, slender body

Similar Species: Mountain Sucker (pg. 130)

<table>
<tr><td align="center">**Bluehead Sucker**</td><td align="center">**Mountain Sucker**</td></tr>
<tr><td align="center"></td><td align="center"></td></tr>
<tr><td align="center">bluish head, lacks notch in corner of mouth</td><td align="center">no blue on head, notch in corner of mouth</td></tr>
</table>

BLUEHEAD SUCKER

Catostomus discobolus

Other Names: none

Habitat: headwater streams to large rivers with medium to strong current and rocky bottoms

Range: middle and upper Colorado River drainage Arizona, Colorado, New Mexico, Utah and Wyoming; in Colorado, it is limited to the Colorado River drainage

Food: algae, invertebrates

Reproduction: spawns in streams during spring and summer

Average Size: 10 to 16 inches

Records: North American—2 pounds, 9 ounces, Strawberry Reservoir, Utah, 1992

Notes: A creature of the current, the Bluehead Sucker requires medium to strong flows and is not found in still water. In rivers or streams with predominantly sand bottoms, look for the bluehead around rocky shoals. Its mouth is lined with ridges of hard cartilage used to scrape algae and invertebrates off rocks. Interestingly, its body shape varies depending on its habitat; blueheads in fast streams have a thin caudal peduncle (the connection from body to tail), while those in slower waters are thicker bodied. In some fisheries, such as the Gunnison River upstream of Blue Mesa Reservoir, it has in recent years been overshadowed by the White and Longnose Suckers, which are native to the East Slope.

Description: greenish-blue to gray back; yellowish sides; white belly; when taken from cloudy water, may have tan back, white to silver sides and belly; blunt snout

Similar Species: Longnose Sucker (pg. 128), Mountain Sucker (pg. 130)

Flannelmouth Sucker	Longnose Sucker	Flannelmouth Sucker	Mountain Sucker
rounded snout barely extends beyond upper lip	long snout distinctly extends beyond upper lip	large, fleshy lower lip lacks distinct notch between upper	thin lower lip with distinct notch between upper

FLANNELMOUTH SUCKER

Catostomidae

Catostomus latipinnis

Other Names: none

Habitat: large rivers and streams; found in varied habitat, including deep pools, riffles, runs, eddies and backwater areas; not usually found in main-lake areas of reservoirs

Range: Colorado River drainage; in Colorado, the middle and upper Colorado River system

Food: algae and other plant matter, aquatic invertebrates

Reproduction: spawns during the spring in streams over gravel bottoms

Average Size: 12 to 24 inches, 2 to 10 pounds

Records: state—4 pounds, 5.5 ounces, Colorado River, 1990; North American—4 pounds, 5 ounces, Flaming Gorge Reservoir, Utah, 1992

Notes: Its streamlined body makes the Flannelmouth Sucker well suited to the turbulent waters of the Colorado River drainage. Though it can be found in a variety of riverine habitats, from deep pools with slow flows to riffles and backwaters, it doesn't do well in reservoir situations. Along with the Bluehead Sucker, the Flannelmouth Sucker appears to fare poorly with competition from Longnose and White Suckers, which have been introduced from their native East Slope range. Cold water released from reservoirs could also play a role in Flannelmouth declines in some tailwater areas.

Description: black, brown to dark olive back; slate to pale
brown sides fading to yellowish or white belly; males
develop red band during spawning season; long snout
protrudes beyond upper lip

Similar Species: White Sucker (pg. 134)

**Longnose
Sucker**

snout extends
well beyond
upper lip

White Sucker

snout barely
extends past
upper lip

LONGNOSE SUCKER

Catostomus catostomus

Other Names: sturgeon, red or redside sucker

Habitat: primarily shallow waters of lakes, rivers and streams; often found in pools and runs with moderate to swift current; tolerates warm and cold water temperatures

Range: Siberia across Canada through Great Lakes to the eastern U.S.; Missouri and Columbia river systems in the West; in Colorado, the Arkansas and South Platte basins, introduced in the Colorado River drainage

Food: algae and other plant matter, crustaceans, insects

Reproduction: spawns in spring at water temperatures from 41 to 59 degrees; adults crowd small tributaries to deposit eggs in shallow water over gravel bottom

Average Size: 15 to 20 inches, 2 pounds

Records: North American—6 pounds, 14 ounces, St. Joseph River, Michigan, 1986

Notes: This widespread northern fish is found in both the Old and New World. Though primarily known as a shallow-water species, it has been reported as deep as 600 feet. Large numbers of Longnose Suckers crowd streams during the spawning run—which typically occurs just before White Suckers enter the same streams to spawn. They have little interest in taking a hook during the spawn but are catchable at other times. Delicious smoked. Serious fish connoisseurs argue that it is superior to the White Sucker in flavor. Hybridizes with native West Slope suckers.

MOUNTAIN SUCKER

RIO GRANDE SUCKER

Description: stout body; back and sides olive to dark gray or brownish with black dots; sometimes mottling across back; underside white; breeding adults develop red-orange band along sides, dark on non-breeding adults

Similar Species: Bluehead Sucker (pg. 124), Rio Grande Sucker

Mountain Sucker	Bluehead Sucker	Mountain Sucker	Rio Grande Sucker
no blue on head, notch in corner of mouth	bluish head, lacks notch in corner of mouth	10 to 12 dorsal rays; also lacks papillae on front upper lip	9 dorsal rays; also has papillae on front upper lip

MOUNTAIN SUCKER

Catostomus platyrhynchus

Other Names: northern and plains mountain sucker

Habitat: riffle areas of clear, cold mountain streams with rock, gravel or sand bottom; occasionally occurs in turbid (cloudy) streams; rarely found in lakes

Range: British Columbia and Alberta to Washington, Utah and Colorado, east to South Dakota; in Colorado, the Green, White, Yampa and upper Colorado basins

Food: algae and other plant matter, invertebrates

Reproduction: matures at 2 to 5 years; scatters sticky eggs over gravel riffles in early to mid-summer when the water temperature passes 50 degrees; eggs hatch in 8 to 14 days

Average Size: up to 8 inches

Records: none

Notes: Look for the Mountain Sucker in small rivers and streams with sand, gravel or rocky bottoms. It prefers modest currents, holding in eddies and pools and around undercut banks. Though it is typically uncommon in lakes, biologists have identified a population in Steamboat Lake. The fish may use its chisel-shaped jaw to scrape algae off rocks. Young Mountain Suckers resemble minnows because the mouth is positioned at the front of the face; it gradually shifts lower as the fish ages. Similar to state-endangered Rio Grande Sucker (*Catostomus plebeius*) found in the Rio Grande from Colorado through Mexico.

Description: bronze to brownish green back and sides; yellowish to white belly; bony, keel-like hump on the back; breeding males turn gray-black with orange belly

Similar Species: Humpback Chub (pg. 52)

Razorback Sucker

Humpback Chub

sucker mouth

forward facing mouth

RAZORBACK SUCKER

Xyrauchen texanus

Other Names: none

Habitat: deep, clear to turbid (cloudy) waters of large rivers and reservoirs; often associated with mud, sand or gravel bottom; most often reported in quiet, soft-bottom areas of river backwaters

Range: Colorado and Gila river basins from Wyoming to Mexico; in Colorado, the lower Yampa River and Colorado River near Grand Junction

Food: plant and animal matter

Reproduction: matures at 3 to 4 years; spawns from November to late June

Average Size: up to 36 inches, 8 to 14 pounds

Records: North American—6 pounds, 4 ounces, Colorado River, Nevada, 1977

Notes: Once so abundant that farmers ground it into livestock feed and fertilizer, the razorback is an amazing, state and federally endangered native Colorado species. Dams, pollution, the arrival of non-native competitors and predators all took their toll on this unique fish. Today, stocking, habitat protection, water flow management and predator reduction programs are helping turn the tide, but the razorback has a long road to recovery. One of North America's largest suckers, it can reach more than 3 feet in length and weights of 12 to 14 pounds; reported to live more than 40 years.

Description: back olive to brown; sides gray to silver; belly white; gray dorsal fin and tail; other fins clear or whitish with limited pigmentation; rounded head; blunt snout

Similar Species: Longnose Sucker (pg. 128)

White Sucker

Longnose Sucker

snout barely extends past upper lip

snout extends well beyond upper lip

WHITE SUCKER
Catostomus commersonii

Other Names: common, coarse-scaled or eastern sucker, black mullet

Habitat: lakes, streams and rivers; in flowing water, adults are often found in pools and runs with low to medium current

Range: Canada through central and eastern U.S., south to a line from New Mexico to South Carolina; statewide in Colorado, to elevations up to 11,500 feet

Food: insects, crustaceans, plant matter

Reproduction: spawns over gravel or coarse sand in April and early May when water temperatures near 52 degrees; adults migrate up small tributaries; in large lakes, spawning may occur along shoreline shallows

Average Size: 12 to 18 inches, 2 to 3 pounds

Records: North American—7 pounds, 4 ounces, Big Round Lake, Wisconsin, 1978

Notes: The White Sucker is widespread and important to the food chain. It provides forage for game fish from Brook Trout to Smallmouth Bass. Not surprisingly, it is a popular baitfish with anglers across its range. A few anglers pursue White Suckers; the meat is bony but delectable when smoked or used in soups, chowders and fish sticks. Native to eastern Colorado, it has become established in the west, where it is thought to have contributed to declines in Bluehead and Flannelmouth Sucker populations.

Description: dark green back, greenish sides often with dark lateral band; belly white to gray; large, forward-facing mouth; lower jaw extends to rear margin of eye

Similar Species: Smallmouth Bass (pg. 138), Spotted Bass (pg. 140)

Largemouth Bass

mouth extends well beyond non-red eye

Smallmouth Bass

mouth does not extend beyond red eye

Spotted Bass

jaw does not extend much beyond eye

136

LARGEMOUTH BASS

Centrarchidae

Micropterus salmoides

Other Names: green bass, green trout, slough bass

Habitat: shallow, fertile, weedy lakes and river backwaters; weedy bays and extensive weedbeds of larger lakes

Range: southern Canada through central U.S. into Mexico, widely introduced; warmwater fisheries in Colorado

Food: small fish, frogs, crayfish, insects, leeches

Reproduction: matures at 3 to 5 years of age; spawns when water temperatures reach 60 degrees, male builds nest in 2 to 8 feet of water, usually on firm bottom in weedy cover; female deposits 2,000 to 40,000 eggs, which the male fans and guards; eggs hatch in about 3 to 4 days; male protects fry until the "brood swarm" disperses

Average Size: 12 to 20 inches, 1 to 5 pounds

Records: state—11 pounds, 6 ounces, Echo Canyon Reservoir, 1997; North American—22 pounds, 4 ounces, Montgomery Lake, Georgia, 1932

Notes: The Largemouth Bass was introduced to Colorado in 1878. From the time it begins feeding 5 to 8 days after hatching, it is an aggressive predator. Young bass eat tiny creatures such as copepods, waterfleas and insect larvae. Before the end of the first growing season, fish are added to the menu. Biologists estimate a bass must eat 4 pounds of forage to produce 1 pound of body weight. Largemouths are typically uncommon in depths greater than 20 feet, but clear-water western reservoirs can provide exceptions.

137

Description: back and sides mottled dark green to bronze or pale gold, often with dark vertical bands; white belly; stout body; large, forward-facing mouth; red eye

Similar Species: Largemouth Bass (pg. 136), Spotted Bass (pg. 140)

Smallmouth Bass	Largemouth Bass	Spotted Bass
mouth does not extend beyond red eye	mouth extends well beyond non-red eye	mouth extends slightly beyond eye

SMALLMOUTH BASS
Micropterus dolomieu

Other Names: bronzeback, brown or redeye bass, redeye

Habitat: clear, cool, streams and rivers with near-permanent flow; clear lakes with gravel or rocky shores, bars and reefs

Range: native to east-central North America, extensively introduced; in Colorado, stocked in lakes statewide

Food: crayfish, small fish (such as chubs, sculpins, stonerollers, darters and suckers), insects, frogs

Reproduction: matures at 4 years; when water temperature reaches mid- to high 60s, male fans out nest in backwater area on gravel; in lakes, nest is often next to a log or boulder; female lays 2,000 to 14,000 eggs, which hatch in about 2 to 7 days; male guards nest and young until fry disperse

Average Size: 10 to 20 inches, 8 ounces to 4 pounds

Records: state—5 pounds, 12 ounces, Navajo Reservoir, 1993; North American—11 pounds, 15 ounces; Dale Hollow Lake, Tennessee, 1955

Notes: A relatively late arrival, the Smallmouth Bass was stocked in Colorado in 1951. In streams, it is often found over silt-free rock or gravel near riffles around rootwads, rocks and other cover—but not in the main current. In lakes, it favors riprap shores and rocky structure offshore. Fry feed on tiny floating animals such as waterfleas; at about 1.5 inches they eat small fish and insect larvae; when bass reach about 3 inches, crayfish become a preferred item and along with fish remain a staple throughout life.

Description: greenish back and upper sides with dark markings and gold reflections; rows of dark spots on whitish lower sides; large mouth; dark spot on gill cover; distinct, sandpaper-like tooth patch on middle of tongue

Similar Species: Largemouth Bass (pg. 136), Smallmouth Bass (pg. 138)

Spotted Bass

Largemouth Bass

Spotted Bass

Smallmouth Bass

jaw does not extend much beyond eye

jaw extends well beyond eye

dark horizontal stripe on side

lacks dark horizontal stripe, may have vertical bars

SPOTTED BASS

Micropterus punctulatus

Other Names: Kentucky bass, spotted black bass, spot

Habitat: warm, slightly turbid (cloudy) streams with year-round flows and main-channel areas of rivers; also found in reservoirs, often in deeper water than other bass

Range: native to south-central U.S., extensively introduced; in Colorado, stocked in the Arkansas drainage

Food: insects, crayfish, fish

Reproduction: matures as early as 1 year, but most spawners are 3- to 4-year-olds; male fans out nest on rock or gravel bottom at water temperatures of 57 to 74 degrees; female deposits from 1,000 to 47,000 eggs; male guards nest but moves off when eggs hatch in about 4 to 5 days—though remains in the vicinity until fry leave the nest

Average Size: 10 to 17 inches, 10 ounces to 3 pounds

Records: state—4 pounds, 7.825 ounces, Valco Ponds, 2005; North American—10 pounds, 4 ounces, Pine Flat Lake, California, 2001

Notes: Stocked in Pueblo Reservoir and found in adjacent waters, the Spotted Bass is fast growing and prolific. Coexists with other bass but is generally found in streams that are too sluggish, warm or turbid (cloudy) for smallmouths, and in areas with too much current for largemouths. Despite this segregation, the arrival of Spotted Bass has in some lakes led to a decline in largemouths and smallmouths. It is thought that spots out-compete other bass for food.

Description: black to dark olive back with purple to emerald reflections; silver sides with dark green or black blotches; back slightly more arched—and depression above eye less pronounced—than White Crappie

Similar Species: White Crappie (pg. 144)

Black Crappie	**White Crappie**	**Black Crappie**	**White Crappie**
usually 7 to 8 spines in dorsal fin	usually 5 to 6 spines in dorsal fin	dorsal fin length equal to distance from dorsal to eye	dorsal fin shorter than distance from eye to dorsal

BLACK CRAPPIE

Centrarchidae

Pomoxis nigromaculatus

Other Names: papermouth, speck, speckled perch, calico bass

Habitat: quiet, clear water of streams and mid-size lakes; often associated with weedgrowth but may roam deep, open basins and flats, particularly during winter

Range: southern Manitoba through Atlantic and southeastern states; widely introduced; common in eastern Colorado

Food: small fish, aquatic insects, zooplankton

Reproduction: matures at 2 to 3 years; spawns in colonies in shallows from May to June when water temperatures reach the high 50s; male sweeps out circular nest, typically on fine gravel or sand bottom next to a plant; female may produce more than 180,000 eggs, which hatch in about 3 to 5 days; male guards nest and fry until young begin feeding

Average Size: 7 to 12 inches, 10 ounces to 1 pound

Records: state—3 pounds, 4 ounces, pond, 1990; North American—6 pounds, Westwego Canal, Louisiana, 1969

Notes: Crappies were introduced to Colorado in 1882 and are pursued year-round by anglers for their sweet-tasting white fillets. The Black Crappie is an aggressive carnivore; adults feed heavily on other fish, including small crappies. Though not noted for its fighting ability, it puts up a good struggle on light tackle. It will hit everything from waxworms to small crankbaits. Actively feeds at night and suspends well off bottom in pursuit of zooplankton and baitfish. Requires clearer water and more vegetation than White Crappies.

Description: greenish to dark olive back with purple to emerald reflections; silvery green to white sides with 7 to 9 dark, vertical bars; anal fin nearly as large as dorsal

Similar Species: Black Crappie (pg. 142)

White Crappie	Black Crappie	White Crappie	Black Crappie

| usually 5 to 6 spines in dorsal fin | usually 7 to 8 spines in dorsal fin | dorsal fin shorter than distance from eye to dorsal | dorsal fin length equal to distance from dorsal to eye |

WHITE CRAPPIE

Pomoxis annularis

Other Names: silver, pale or ringed crappie, papermouth

Habitat: slightly turbid (cloudy) streams, rivers and mid-size lakes; prefers less vegetation than Black Crappie

Range: North Dakota south and east to Gulf and Atlantic, except peninsular Florida; introduced in eastern Colorado

Food: aquatic insects, small fish, plankton

Reproduction: typically matures at 2 years; spawns on firm sand or gravel in May and June when water temperature approaches 60 degrees; male fans out nest, often near a log or plant roots; female deposits from 3,000 to 15,000 eggs, which hatch in 3 to 5 days; male guards eggs and fry

Average Size: 6 to 12 inches, 8 to 16 ounces

Records: state—4 pounds, 3.75 ounces, Northglenn Lake, 1975; North American—5 pounds, 3 ounces; Enid Dam, Mississippi, 1957

Notes: Popular with panfish fans thanks to its flavorful fillets, the White Crappie is often found in large but relatively loose schools, suspended off bottom and away from weeds or structure. In reservoirs with standing timber, however, it may relate to this woody cover. Actively feeds at night and during winter. Due to its tolerance of turbid (cloudy) water, there is some indication of a positive relationship between the Common Carp and White Crappie. In streams, look for it in pools or backwaters away from the main channel; it avoids cool, spring-fed inflows and extremely cloudy water.

Description: round, flat body; spines in dorsal and anal fins; small mouth; dark olive to green on back, blending to silver-gray, copper, orange, purple or brown on sides with 5 to 9 dark, vertical bars that may fade with age; yellow underside and copper breast, which intensifies on spawning males; large, dark gill spot; dark spot on rear margin of dorsal fin

Similar Species: Green Sunfish (pg. 148), Pumpkinseed (pg. 152)

Bluegill

Green Sunfish

Bluegill

Pumpkinseed

small mouth   large mouth   dark gill spot   orange crescent

Bluegill

Pumpkinseed

dark spot on dorsal fin   no dark spot

BLUEGILL
Lepomis macrochirus

Other Names: bream, copperbelly, pond perch

Habitat: streams and lakes with weedy bays or shorelines

Range: southern Canada into Mexico; introduced across much of southern and eastern Colorado

Food: insects, small fish, leeches, snails, zooplankton, algae

Reproduction: matures at about 2 years; spawns from May to early August at water temperatures of 67 to 80 degrees; "parental" male excavates nest in gravel or coarse sand, often in shallow weeds, in colonies of up to 50 other nests; a smaller non-nesting "cuckholder" male (exhibiting female behavior and coloration) may dart into the nest and fertilize the eggs; after spawning, the parental male chases the female away and guards nest until fry disperse

Average Size: 6 to 9½ inches, 5 to 12 ounces

Records: state—2 pounds, 4 ounces, Hollenbeck Reservoir, 1988; North American—4 pounds, 12 ounces, Ketona Lake, Alabama, 1950

Notes: One of the most widely distributed panfish in North America, the Bluegill is a favorite of anglers young and old for its tenacious fight and excellent table quality. Small fish are easy to catch near docks in summer. Larger "bulls" favor deep weeds much of the year; during the spawn, colonies are targeted and sometimes overfished. Hybridizes with other sunfish. Has acute daytime vision for feeding on small prey items, but sees poorly in low light.

Description: dark green back; dark olive to bluish sides; yellow or whitish belly; scales flecked with yellow creating a brassy appearance; dark gill spot has a pale margin

Similar Species: Bluegill (pg. 146)

Green Sunfish

large mouth

Bluegill

small mouth

GREEN SUNFISH

Lepomis cyanellus

Other Names: black perch, blue-spotted sunfish, sand bass

Habitat: warm, weedy shallow lakes and the backwaters of slow-moving streams

Range: most of the U.S. into Mexico excluding Florida and the Rocky Mountains; native to the east slope of Colorado, introduced elsewhere

Food: aquatic and terrestrial insects, crustaceans, small fish

Reproduction: beginning in May, male fans out nest on coarse sand or gravel, often in less than 1 foot of water, near cover—often beneath overhanging limbs; male may grunt to lure female into nest; after spawning, male guards nest and fans eggs; spawns in water temperatures from 60 to 80 degrees, capable of producing two broods per season

Average Size: 5 to 8 inches, less than 12 ounces

Records: state—tie: 1 pound, 5 ounces, Big Thompson Pond/gravel pit, 1997/2001; North American—2 pounds, 2 ounces, Stockton Lake, Missouri, 1971

Notes: The Green Sunfish is easy to catch but not a widely popular sportfish because of its small size. Highly prolific, it may overpopulate a lake with stunted 3-inch bait robbers. Tolerant of high siltation and low oxygen levels, it thrives in warm, weedy lakes and backwaters. It also withstands drought conditions and is often among the last survivors in the pools of intermittent streams. Hybridizes with Bluegill and Pumpkinseed producing larger, more voracious offspring.

Description: bluish green back fading to orange; about 30 orange or red spots on sides of males, brown spots on females; orange pelvic and anal fins; black gill spot has light margin

Similar Species: Bluegill (pg. 146), Green Sunfish (pg. 148), Pumpkinseed (pg. 152)

Orangespotted Sunfish

light margin on gill spot

Bluegill

gill spot lacks light margin

Pumpkinseed

orange or red crescent on gill

Orangespotted Sunfish

hard spines higher than soft rays

Green Sunfish

hard spines shorter than soft rays

ORANGESPOTTED SUNFISH

Centrarchidae

Lepomis humilis

Other Names: orangespot, dwarf or pygmy sunfish

Habitat: ponds and lakes with open to moderately weedy areas; quiet pools and backwaters of rivers and streams

Range: Great Lakes through Mississippi River basin to Gulf States; in Colorado, the Arkansas and South Platte basins

Food: insects, crustaceans, small fish

Reproduction: matures in 2 to 3 years; spawns May through August when water temperatures reach mid to high 60s; male fans out nest on gravel or coarse sand in shallow water; colonial nesters; male guards nest after spawning until eggs hatch, typically in about 5 days

Average Size: 3 to 4 inches, 4 ounces

Records: none

Notes: Native to eastern Colorado, this brightly colored little sunfish is occasionally taken by anglers but is too small to be a significant sportfish. Still, it is important as forage species for other game fish and may be important for mosquito larvae control in some areas. It prefers clear streams with rock bottoms but tolerates turbid (cloudy) water and slight pollution better than many other sunfish, making it well suited for small lakes in agricultural areas. Often found in the pools of prairie streams, it avoids areas with strong, fast current.

Description: back brown to olive; sides speckled with orange, yellow, blue and green spots with 7 to 10 vertical bands; chest and belly yellow or orange; black gill spot has light margin with orange or red crescent

Similar Species: Bluegill (pg. 146), Green Sunfish (pg. 148), Orangespotted Sunfish (pg. 150)

Pumpkinseed

orange or red crescent on gill flap

Bluegill

gill flap lacks orange or red margin

Orangespotted Sunfish

light margin on gill flap

Pumpkinseed

long, pointed pectoral fin

Green Sunfish

rounded pectoral fin

PUMPKINSEED

Lepomis gibbosus

Other Names: punky, yellow or round sunfish, bream

Habitat: weedy ponds, clear lakes and slow-moving streams; prefers slightly cooler water than the Bluegill

Range: native to eastern and central North America, widely introduced; impoundments in eastern Colorado

Food: insects, snails, fish, leeches, small amounts of vegetation

Reproduction: matures in 2 to 3 years; spawns late May to August, starting when water temperatures reach 55 to 63 degrees; male builds nest in colony on coarse sand, gravel or soft bottom among weeds in shallow water; female may produce 4,000 to 7,000 eggs per season; after spawning, female leaves the nest, which is aggressively guarded by the male; multiple broods per year are common

Average Size: 6 to 8 inches, 6 to 10 ounces

Records: state—none; North American—2 pounds, 4 ounces, North Saluda River, South Carolina, 1997

Notes: Named for the orange, seed-shaped spot on its gill, the Pumpkinseed often schools under submerged logs or deadfalls and around docks. It is aggressive, easy to catch on small natural and artificial baits and fine table fare. Large fish often feed along edges of deep weeds during the day and settle to bottom at night. Hybridization with other sunfish is common, as is stunting. In stunted populations, it may reproduce when only 2½ inches long. Eats insects and fish, also uses specialized teeth to feed on snails.

Description: brown to olive green back and sides with dark spots and overall bronze appearance; red eye; thicker, heavier body than other sunfish; large mouth

Similar Species: Bluegill (pg. 146), Green Sunfish (pg. 148), Pumpkinseed (pg. 152), Sacramento Perch (pg. 156)

Rock Bass

large mouth extends to eye

Bluegill

small mouth does not extend to eye

Rock Bass

spotted sides lack vertical bars

Sacramento Perch

sides have blotchy vertical bars

Rock Bass

6 spines in anal fin

Green Sunfish

3 spines in anal fin

Pumpkinseed

3 spines in anal fin

ROCK BASS

Ambloplites rupestris

Other Names: redeye, goggle eye, rock sunfish

Habitat: vegetation on firm to rocky bottom in clear-water lakes and medium-size streams

Range: southern Canada through central and eastern U.S. to northern edge of Gulf states; in Colorado, introduced in the upper Arkansas and Republican drainages

Food: prefers crayfish, but eats aquatic insects and small fish

Reproduction: matures at 2 to 3 years; spawns in spring at water temperatures from high 60s to 70s; male fans out 8- to 10-inch diameter nest in 1 to 5 feet of water, on coarse sand or gravel bottom, often next to a boulder or in weeds; male guards eggs and fry

Average Size: 8 to 10 inches, 8 ounces to 1 pound

Records: state—1 pound, 1.25 ounces, Ramah Reservoir, 1979; North American—3 pounds, York R., Ontario, 1974

Notes: Found in eastern Colorado, the chunky Rock Bass is a secretive fish that frequents weedbeds associated with rocky, sandy or gravel bottoms. It has the chameleon-like ability to rapidly change colors to match its surroundings. Though the Rock Bass is hard-fighting and good-tasting, it is seldom targeted by anglers. It may feed throughout the day but is most active at dusk and during the night.

Description: blackish back; with about seven dark, irregular vertical bars; large mouth

Similar Species: Black Crappie (pg. 142), White Crappie (pg. 144), Rock Bass (pg. 154), Smallmouth Bass (pg. 138)

Sacramento Perch
12 or 13 spines in dorsal fin

Black, White Crappie
10 or fewer spines in dorsal

Smallmouth Bass
10 or fewer spines in dorsal

Sacramento Perch
sides have blotchy vertical bars

Rock Bass
spotted sides lack vertical bars

SACRAMENTO PERCH

Archoplites interruptus

Other Names: none

Habitat: weedy lakes, ponds and slow-flowing streams

Range: native to California's Sacramento-San Joaquin, Pajaro and Salinas river drainages and Clear Lake; in Colorado, introduced in the Cache la Poudre and South Platte drainages, along with other waters

Food: small fish, insects, crustaceans

Reproduction: matures in 2 to 3 years; does not build a nest; spawns May through August at water temperatures of 71 to 75 degrees; males establish territories in shallow water; eggs are scattered over algae-covered rocks or plant roots; some researchers have noted egg-guarding behavior by males, while other studies have found no parental care

Average Size: less than 12 inches and 14 ounces

Records: state—1 pound, 14 ounces, Banner Lakes, 1974; North American—4 pounds, 9 ounces, Pyramid Lake, Nevada, 1971

Notes: Despite its name, the Sacramento Perch is actually a member of the Sunfish family—and the only one native west of the Rockies. The introduction of non-native species has led to declines in its home range. Able to tolerate higher salt concentrations and alkalinity than many freshwater fish, it as been introduced in select waters across the West, including some in Colorado. Not a schooler or particularly aggressive, it is often hard to catch on hook and line.

157

Description: bluish to dark olive-green back; silver on sides with about 7 dark, horizontal streaks; white belly; base of tongue has two parallel patches of teeth; usually 11 to 12 soft rays in second dorsal fin; body depth less than one-third length to base of tail (as opposed to deeper-bodied White Bass); two spines on gill cover

Similar Species: White Bass (pg. 160), Wiper (pg. 162)

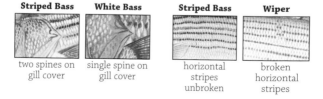

Striped Bass	**White Bass**	**Striped Bass**	**Wiper**
two spines on gill cover	single spine on gill cover	horizontal stripes unbroken	broken horizontal stripes

STRIPED BASS

Morone saxatilis

Moronidae

Other Names: striper, linesides, rockfish

Habitat: fresh- or saltwater; schools roam clear water along shorelines and bays, but are also found in open water

Range: native to the East Coast of North America and parts of the Gulf of Mexico; widely introduced; inadvertently released in Colorado when pure strain Striped Bass were mistaken for White Bass or Wipers

Food: fish, insects, crustaceans

Reproduction: matures from age two (males) to three or four (females); migrates into rivers and to reservoir shoals or headwaters in spring and summer in water temperatures of 60 to 68 degrees; spawns in moving water; successful reproduction requires constant current because eggs must remain off bottom until hatching—usually in 36 to 75 hours

Average Size: 22 to 36 inches, 5 to 20 pounds

Records: state—12 pounds, 13 ounces, CF & I Reservoir No. 2, 1984; North American—67 pounds, 1 ounce, Colorado River, Arizona, 1997

Notes: The Striped Bass is highly adaptable; it can survive in saltwater, freshwater and brackish conditions in water up to about 95 degrees. Given abundant forage, it can reach nearly 30 inches in length and 10 pounds in weight in five growing seasons. Maximum weights of more than 100 pounds are possible, but fish over 50 are rare.

Description: bright silver; 6 to 8 distinct, uninterrupted black stripes on each side; front hard-spined portion of dorsal fin separated from soft-rayed rear section; lower jaw protrudes beyond snout

Similar Species: Wiper (pg. 162), Striped Bass (pg. 158)

White Bass	**Wiper**	**White Bass**	**Striped Bass**
single tooth patch on tongue	two rows of teeth on tongue	single spine on gill cover	two spines on gill cover

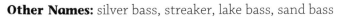

WHITE BASS

Morone chrysops

Other Names: silver bass, streaker, lake bass, sand bass

Habitat: large lakes and rivers with relatively clear water

Range: Great Lakes region to the eastern seaboard, through the southeast to the Gulf; introduced in warmwater fisheries in eastern and southwestern Colorado

Food: small fish, insects, crustaceans

Reproduction: spawns in late spring to early summer at water temperatures of 55 to 79 degrees, in open water over gravel beds or rubble 6 to 10 feet deep; a single female may produce more than 500,000 eggs

Average Size: 9 to 18 inches, 8 ounces to 2 pounds

Records: state—4 pounds, 7 ounces, Blue Lake, 1963; North American—6 pounds, 7 ounces, Saginaw Bay, Michigan, 1989

Notes: The White Bass is a willing striker and hard fighter that favors deep pools in streams and open water in large lakes. It travels and hunts in large schools that are often spotted near the surface; watch for seagulls feeding on frightened baitfish that flee these marauding predators. White Bass fillets are of good table quality; like most species, the flavor and texture can be preserved if the fish are quickly put on ice.

Description: dark gray or silvery blue body with 6 to 8 thick, dark horizontal stripes broken above and below lateral line; deep, flat body; small head and distinct back arch

Similar Species: Striped Bass (pg. 158), White Bass (pg. 160)

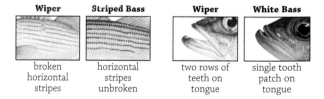

Wiper	Striped Bass	Wiper	White Bass
broken horizontal stripes	horizontal stripes unbroken	two rows of teeth on tongue	single tooth patch on tongue

WIPER

Morone saxatilis x Morone chrysops

Moronidae

Other Names: whiterock, sunshine bass

Habitat: large, warmwater reservoirs and rivers with an abundant forage base of small fish

Range: none, a hybrid of the striped bass and white bass; widely introduced from Florida and East Coast to Oregon and California; stocked in east slope drainages of Colorado

Food: fish such as shad, sunfish and silversides; also insects, crustaceans

Reproduction: believed not to reproduce in Colorado though limited reproduction has been reported in other states

Average Size: 24 inches, 5 to 6 pounds

Records: state—26 pounds, 15 ounces, Pueblo Reservoir, 2004; North American—27 pounds, 5 ounces, Greer's Ferry Lake, Arkansas, 1997

Notes: A popular sportfish introduced in eastern Colorado in the early 1980s, the Wiper is a hybrid cross of White Bass and Striped Bass. Thanks to a natural phenomenon known as hybrid vigor (used to describe the increased physical strength of a cross between two related species), the Wiper is a fast-growing, aggressive, hard-fighting game fish. Often seen busting baitfish in large schools at the surface over deep water. Small groups patrol shoreline shallows when water temperatures exceed 60 degrees in the spring, offering anglers white-knuckle battles on light tackle.

PLAINS KILLIFISH

MOSQUITOFISH

Description: olive-brown back; sides tan, yellow or black fading to yellowish white underside; sides marked by series of thin, dark bars; broad, flat head; breeding males may turn bright yellow and red

Similar Species: Mosquitofish

Plains Killifish	Mosquitofish
vertical bars on sides; front of dorsal fin slightly ahead of anal fin	sides lack bars; anal fin mostly to entirely ahead of dorsal fin

164

PLAINS KILLIFISH

Fundulus kansae

Other Names: none

Habitat: shallow streams, often with sand or silt bottom; favors quiet water adjacent to shoals, channels and banks; also found in backwaters; tolerates some current

Range: native to Mississippi River and Gulf Slope drainages from Missouri to Wyoming south to Texas; introduced elsewhere; in Colorado, native to warmwater streams in the Arkansas, South Platte and Republican basins, introduced in the Colorado and Gunnison rivers

Food: aquatic invertebrates, algae

Reproduction: matures at about 2 years; spawns May through July when water temperatures reach 80 degrees; males do not establish territories but become aggressive toward other males; spawns in pairs, commonly burying eggs in sand bottom

Average Size: 2 to 3 inches

Records: none

Notes: A common species on the western Great Plains, the Plains Killifish can survive in water less than an inch deep and tolerate water temperatures approaching 90 degrees. Known to survive in areas where farm runoff has left the bottom covered with oxygen-burning organic matter. Very similar to the Western Mosquitofish (*Gambusia affinis*), a member of the Poeciliidae family that gives birth to live young and is widely stocked for mosquito control.

GLOSSARY

adipose fin a small, fleshy fin without rays, located on the midline of the fish's back between the dorsal fin and the tail

air bladder a balloon-like organ located in the gut area of a fish, used to control buoyancy—and in the respiration of some species such as gar; also called "swim bladder" or "gas bladder"

alevin a newly hatched fish that still has its yolk sac

anadromous a fish that hatches in freshwater, migrates to the ocean, the re-enters streams or rivers from the sea (or large inland body of water) to spawn

anal fin a single fin located on the underside near the tail

annulus marks or rings on the scales, spine, vertebrae or otoliths that scientists use to determine a fish's age

anterior toward the front of a fish, opposite of posterior

bands horizontal markings running lengthwise along the side of a fish

barbel thread-like sensory structures on a fish's head often near the mouth, commonly called "whiskers;" used for taste or smell

bars vertical markings on the side of a fish

benthic organisms living in or on the bottom

brood swarm a large group or "cloud" of young fish such as Black Bullheads

carnivore a predatory fish that feeds on other fish (also called a piscivore) or animals

catadromous a fish that lives in freshwater and migrates into salt-water to spawn, such as the American Eel

caudal fin the tail or tail fin

caudal peduncle the portion of the fish's body located between the anal fin and the beginning of the tail

coldwater referring to a species or environment; in fish, often a species of trout or salmon found in water that rarely exceeds 70 degrees; also used to describe a lake or river according to average summer temperature

copepod a small (less than 2 mm) crustacean that is part of the zooplankton community

crustacean a crayfish, water flea, crab or other animal belonging to group of mostly aquatic species that have paired antennae, jointed legs and an exterior skeleton (exoskeleton); common food for many fish

dorsal relating to the top of the fish, on or near the back; opposite of the ventral, or lower, part of the fish

dorsal fin the fin or fins located along the top of a fish's back

eddy a circular water current, often created by an obstruction

epilimnion the warm, oxygen-rich upper layer of water in a thermally stratified lake

exotic a foreign species, not native to a watershed, such as the Zebra Mussel

fingerling a juvenile fish, generally 1 to 10 inches in length, in its first year of life

fork length the overall length of a fish from the mouth to the deepest part of the tail notch

fry recently hatched young fish that have already absorbed their yolk sacs

game fish a species regulated by laws for recreational fishing

gills organs used in aquatic respiration (breathing)

gill cover large bone covering the fish's gills, also called opercle or operculum

gill flap also called ear flap; fleshy projection on the back edge of the gill cover of some fish such as Bluegill

gill raker a comblike projection from the gill arch

harvest fish that are caught and kept by recreational or commercial anglers

hypolimnion bottom layer of the water column in a thermally stratified lake (common in summer), is usually depleted of oxygen by decaying matter, and inhospitable to most fish

ichthyologist a scientist who studies fish

invertebrates animals without backbones, such as insects, crayfish, leeches and earthworms

lateral line a series of pored scales along the side of a fish that contain organs used to detect vibrations

littoral zone the part of a lake that is less than 15 feet in depth; this important and often vulnerable area holds the majority of aquatic plants, is a primary area used by young fish, and offers essential spawning habitat for most warmwater fishes such as Walleye and Largemouth Bass

mandible lower jaw

maxillary upper jaw

milt semen of a male fish that fertilizes the female's eggs during the spawning process

mollusk an invertebrate with a smooth, soft body such as a clam or a snail, often having an outer shell

native an indigenous or naturally occurring species

omnivore a fish or animal that eats plants and animal matter

otolith calcium concentration found in the inner ear of fish; used to determine age of some fish; also called ear bone

opercle the bone covering the gills, also called the gill cover or operculum

panfish small freshwater game fish that can be fried whole in a pan, such as Black Crappie, Bluegill and Yellow Perch

pectoral fins paired fins on the side of the fish located just behind the gills

pelagic fish species that live in open water, in the food-rich upper layer of the column; not associated with the bottom

pelvic fins paired fins located below or behind the pectoral fins on the bottom (ventral portion) of the fish

pheromone a chemical scent secreted as a means of communication between members of the same species

piscivore a predatory fish that mainly eats other fish

planktivore a fish that feeds on plankton

plankton floating or weakly swimming aquatic plants and animals, including larval fish, that drift with the current; often eaten by fish; individual organisms are called plankters

plankton bloom a marked increase in the amount of plankton due to favorable conditions such as nutrients and light

range the geographic region in which a species is found

ray, hard stiff fin support; resembles a spine but is jointed

ray, soft flexible fin support, sometimes branched

redd a nest like depression made by a male or female fish during the spawn, often refers to nest of trout and salmon species

riprap rock or concrete used to protect a lakeshore or river's bank from erosion

roe fish eggs

scales small, flat plates covering the outer skin of many fish

Secchi disc an 8- to 12-inch-diameter, black-and-white circular disc used to measure water clarity; scientists record the average depth at which the disc disappears from sight when lowered into the water

silt small, easily disturbed bottom particles smaller than sand but larger than clay

siltation the accumulation of soil particles

spawning the process of fish reproduction; involves females laying eggs and males fertilizing them to produce young fish

spine stiff, non-jointed structures found along with soft rays in some fins

spiracle an opening on the posterior portion of the head above and behind the eye

standard length length of the fish from the mouth to the end of the vertebral column

stocking the purposeful, artificial introduction of a fish species into a body of water

substrate bottom composition of a lake, stream or river

subterminal mouth a mouth below the snout of the fish

swim bladder see air bladder

tailrace area of water immediately downstream of a dam or power plant

thermocline middle layer of water in a stratified lake, typically oxygen rich, characterized by a sharp drop in temperature; often the lowest depth at which fish can be routinely found

terminal mouth forward facing

total length the length of the fish from the mouth to the tail compressed to its fullest length

tributary a stream that feeds into another stream, river or lake

turbid cloudy; water clouded by suspended sediments or plant matter that limits visibility and the passage of light

velocity the speed of water flowing in a stream or river

vent the opening at the end of the digestive tract

ventral the underside of the fish

vertebrate an animal with a backbone

warmwater a non-salmonid species of fish that lives in water that routinely exceeds 70 degrees; also used to describe a lake or river according to average summer temperature

yolk the part of an egg containing food for the developing fish

zooplankton the animal component of plankton; tiny animals that float or swim weakly; common food for small fish

INDEX

REFERENCES

Much of the information for this book came from research presentations, the U.S. Fish and Wildlife Service, U.S. Geological Survey, and state, provincial and university departments of conservation, fisheries and wildlife, most notably the Colorado Division of Wildlife. Other valuable sources of information include the titles listed below:

Bosanko, David. 2007
Fish of Minnesota
Adventure Publications, Inc.

Hanophy, Wendy. 2006
Native Fish of Colorado's Eastern Plains
Colorado Division of Wildlife

Pflieger, William L. 1997
Fishes of Missouri, The
Missouri Department of Conservation

Sternberg, Dick. 1987
Freshwater Gamefish of North America
Cy DeCosse, Inc.

ABOUT THE AUTHOR

Dan Johnson is an author and lifelong student of freshwater fish and fishing. For nearly two decades he has brought North American anglers breaking news on the latest scientific research, fishing techniques and related technology. Dan is a longtime attendee of American Fisheries Society annual conferences and related symposia. He is a syndicated weekly newspaper columnist, and has published more than 200 feature articles nationwide in the pages of *North American Fisherman*, *Walleye In-Sider* and other publications. Dan has also made numerous fishing-related television appearances on ESPN2. Above all, he is a passionate angler who enjoys spending time on the water with his family, patterning fish behavior and observing how these fascinating creations interact with one another in the underwater web of life. He resides in Cambridge, Minnesota, with wife, Julie, and children, Emily, Jacob and Joshua.